fast
COOKING

JAMES MARTIN

fast COOKING

PHOTOGRAPHY BY TARA FISHER

Quadrille
PUBLISHING

To my mother – you are the inspiration for everything I do.

Publishing director: Jane O'Shea
Creative director: Helen Lewis
Project editor: Laura Gladwin
Art direction & design: Gabriella Le Grazie
Photographer: Tara Fisher
Food stylists: Chris Start, Sam Head
Props stylist: Liz Belton
Production: Vincent Smith, James Finan

First published in 2013 by
Quadrille Publishing Limited
Alhambra House
27–31 Charing Cross Road
London WC2H 0LS
www.quadrille.co.uk

This edition produced for The Book People, Hall Wood Avenue,
Haydock, St Helens, WA11 9UL

Text © 2013 James Martin
Photography © 2013 Tara Fisher
Design and layout © 2013 Quadrille Publishing Limited

Cataloguing in Publication Data: a catalogue record for
this book is available from the British Library.

978 1 84949 359 8

Printed in Germany

INTRODUCTION

Doing a show like Saturday Kitchen means that I've quickly got used to fast cooking. Most dishes have to be cooked within 7 or 8 minutes, and the pressure is really on. So when I was asked to do a book on fast food I jumped at the chance, and of course it made a great partner for my last one, Slow Cooking.

As you probably know, I grew up a farmer's kid, and because of that, British food and its seasons are central to my ethos of cooking. It's so important to get not only the best flavour, but also the best value, and buying food in season means that it's at its most abundant, and therefore at its cheapest. We can look forward to the arrival of seasonal foods such as Jersey Royal potatoes and asparagus, and many others can be added to the long list of tasty treats.

But it's not all about waiting for the best produce: the dishes in this book make good use of the vast array of good-quality ready-made food available on supermarket shelves. What I've tried to do is to give you clever shortcuts to ease the burden of cooking. Shop-bought stocks are great, ready-made custard can be made into a simple passion fruit soufflé that takes just minutes (page 191), and instant mashed potatoes transform smoked haddock fish cakes (page 86) into a fast supper. We all do it, and chefs who say they make everything at home and simmer beef bones for 48 hours to make stock aren't telling the truth! Spending 18 hours a day in a restaurant kitchen teaches you a thing or two about not cooking that kind of food at the end of your long day. Let's face it, we're all leading busy lives, and if I'm honest, this is the food I really cook at home.

Many of the dishes have been inspired by my trips away. One of the great joys of this job is being able to travel and discover food scenes and recipes to bring back to the UK. There are a few dishes I came across in the US, such as the Whoopie Cakes on page 203 from Dumbo in New York City (it's an acronym for Down Under the Manhattan Bridge Overpass), and the Ice Box Cake on page 164 from the bakery that features in the TV show Sex *and the* City. *We have much to learn from our friends across the water when it comes to fast cooking – it's not just doughnuts and burgers! Further afield, I had one of the best street food dishes I've ever tasted in Singapore: the chilli crab on page 76, a dish that's really worth trying. In the middle of the Indian Ocean I had a lunch of seared tuna with coconut chilli chutney (page 106) that was so good I went back to the same place to eat it more than half a dozen times! Closer to home, there are dishes I picked up during the time I spent training in France when I was younger. Using sorrel in a quick sauce was one of the first things I learned, even before learning to say* oui *or* non.

Other dishes are inspired by the time I've spent presenting Saturday Kitchen, *which I think has to be the best job in any kitchen. I get a small insight into all the great chefs of the world, a peek into their kitchens and a good look at the way food is heading. Thomas Keller, Michel Roux Snr and Daniel Boulud are just a few of the chefs I've been commis chef for on the show over the years. The ingredients they bring are inspiring too, such as fantastic maple syrup, or new cheeses I've never tried before, like the Ogleshield cheese that's made from Jersey cows' milk on a small farm in Somerset. Hints, techniques and dishes from them and other chefs are dotted around the book for you to enjoy – as well as my own of course! And for that I want to thank the team who make the show, the chefs from around the world who continue to join me on it, and the great guests who've come along too.*

But cooking at home is what this book is all about: simple suppers made in minutes, without compromising flavour. Whether you've got people coming for dinner and not much time to cook, or just need a quick and tasty after-work supper, there are plenty of ideas here. They're all simple dishes that are achievable by every home cook. Speaking of home, all these dishes were cooked and the photographs taken at my house, along with my small team of merry helpers. Well, I say merry – they started off that way, but by the end we all looked a bit harrassed, mainly because of all the washing up! But we did it without using fancy equipment; there's no liquid nitrogen, foams or gels here. I'll leave that for other books – this is just quick, honest grub. It's not going to cost a fortune to get the ingredients, nor will you have to trawl the internet in search of ingredients from far-flung places. There are more than 100 dishes here for you to enjoy: all of them can be cooked in less than 20 minutes, and they all taste far, far better than the convenience food that many of us have become used to. They're all adaptable, too: in Starters you'll find lots of ideas for light meals and lunches, and in Mains you'll find that all the accompaniments you need for a complete meal are built in, but you can leave these out if you want something lighter, or if you're serving a starter beforehand. You can think of the recipes as blueprints to which you can add your own variations, and I've suggested where you can do this in the introductions.

So off you go – get down to the shops and have a go! I hope you enjoy using this book as much as I've enjoyed writing it.

Happy fast cooking,

ASPARAGUS WITH SWEET SOY & SESAME

This is a must when asparagus is in season around the end of April, as it's one of the true food delights – but, like anything good, it doesn't last forever: just seven or eight weeks. I love the saltiness of soy sauce, which goes so well with the charred asparagus. Tamari is a tasty type of soy that's used in Japanese cooking and sushi, and you could use that here too.

Serves 4

2 large bunches asparagus
50ml olive oil
15g white sesame seeds
15g black sesame seeds
100ml sweet soy or tamari sauce
sea salt and freshly ground black pepper

1 If necessary, snap the woody bases off the asparagus stems. Toss the asparagus in the oil and season with salt and pepper.

2 Heat a large griddle pan until hot. Add the asparagus and cook for 2–3 minutes, or until just tender.

3 Meanwhile, toast the sesame seeds in a dry frying pan until nutty and fragrant. When the asparagus is cooked, coat in the soy sauce, sprinkle over the sesame seeds and serve immediately.

Serves 4

1 banana shallot
25g butter
100g watercress
250g frozen peas
750ml chicken stock, hot
100g ready-made croutons
50g crème fraîche
sea salt and freshly ground black pepper

1 Dice the banana shallot. Melt the butter in a large saucepan, add the shallot and cook gently for 2–3 minutes, until softened.

2 Add the watercress and peas and cover with the hot stock. Season with salt and pepper and bring to the boil.

3 Transfer to a large food processor or blender and blitz until smooth. Pour into warm serving bowls and serve topped with croutons and crème fraîche.

This may be made with frozen peas, but don't let that worry you – they're a great shortcut to a vibrant green colour and flavour. Don't overcook it, as you'll end up with a mushy-pea flavour and not the bright, fresh taste we want. Watercress is one of the ultimate super-foods, and I think it's miles better than rocket. The cold, fresh spring water it needs to grow helps the leaves stay nice and crisp.

GREEN PEA & WATERCRESS SOUP

5 eggs
25g flour
25g panko breadcrumbs
vegetable oil, for deep-frying
100g radishes
4 little gem lettuces
1 small bunch fresh chives
8 slices ready-cooked
crispy bacon
sea salt and freshly
ground black pepper

1 Bring a pan of water to the boil, add 4 of the eggs and cook for 5½ minutes. Drain, then plunge into iced water.

2 Lightly beat the remaining egg. Peel the boiled eggs, then coat them in flour, the beaten egg and the breadcrumbs.

3 Heat the oil to 160°C/320°F in a deep-fryer, add the eggs and cook for 1–2 minutes, until golden brown. Remove and drain on kitchen paper.

4 Meanwhile, thinly slice the radishes and separate the lettuce leaves. Cut the chives into short lengths. Mix together the lettuce, chives and radishes and crumble over the bacon slices.

5 Divide the salad leaves among the plates and top each one with an egg. Season with salt and pepper, and serve.

Deep-fried eggs may look like hard work, but they're so simple. The cooking time is important, and 5½ minutes is perfect for a soft-boiled medium egg – trust me, I've done it many times over the years! You end up with different textures from the crispy outside and the soft egg yolk, which makes a nice dressing. Little gem lettuce is one of the best-tasting leaves at the supermarket. To really crisp the leaves up, plunge them into ice-cold water before serving.

DEEP-FRIED SOFT-BOILED EGG WITH CRISPY BACON SALAD

Serves 4
1 x 400g tin pear halves
4 red endives
50g pecorino cheese
100g walnuts

For the dressing
1 fresh chive sprig
1 fresh mint sprig
1 fresh flat-leaf parsley sprig
50ml mayonnaise
50ml buttermilk
½ tsp garlic powder
½ tsp onion seeds
juice of ½ lemon
sea salt and freshly
ground black pepper

1 Drain the pears and pat them dry with kitchen paper. Heat a griddle pan until hot, then grill the pears for 2 minutes on each side. Remove and set aside.

2 Trim the endives and cut them into quarters lengthways. Shave the pecorino and chop the walnuts roughly.

3 Make the dressing. Chop the chives, mint and parsley, then whisk together all the dressing ingredients in a small bowl.

4 Place the endive and pears on serving plates and sprinkle with pecorino and walnuts. Drizzle with dressing and serve.

Endive has a bitter flavour that really works in salads. Try to get young endive, as the older, green-topped ones are better cooked. Buttermilk can be found in nearly all supermarkets, and I use it in many things, from ice creams to panna cottas. The slightly acidic flavour is great in dressings, and this is a really handy one to know.

ENDIVE, CHARRED PEAR, PECORINO & WALNUT SALAD

Serves 4

½ red cabbage
25ml sherry vinegar
25ml olive oil
2 balls (approximately 250g)
Hampshire mozzarella
12 slices Parma ham
sea salt and freshly
ground black pepper

1 Finely shred the red cabbage – a food processor with a slicing attachment makes this easier.

2 Mix together the cabbage, sherry vinegar and olive oil and season with salt and pepper.

3 Tear the mozzarella into 8 pieces. Divide the cabbage salad among the serving plates, top with pieces of mozzarella and Parma ham, and serve.

I prefer red cabbage thinly sliced in a salad to braised. Leave it in the dressing for a few minutes so that the oil and vinegar slightly wilts it. I'm lucky, as the mozzarella I use is from just down the road at Laverstoke Park, but supermarkets sell it too, and you can buy it online. Buy it as fresh as possible and use it straight away, as it starts to deteriorate as you keep it. If you can find burrata, that works well too. It's often made from mozzarella trimmings mixed with cream, and it tastes brilliant.

HAMPSHIRE MOZZARELLA WITH RED CABBAGE & PARMA HAM

BAKED GOAT'S CHEESE WITH RED ONION JAM

Red onions have a sweetness that makes them perfect for a quick jam that cuts though the chalkiness of the cheese. I've done individual ones here, but a whole cheese brought to the table is a great sharing dish. Make sure the goat's cheese is one that melts when grilled or cooked (these will usually have a rind). The best part is the bits the cook gets to scrape off the tray!

Serves 4

4 x 50g goat's cheeses, with rind (or 1 x 200g log sliced into 4)

4 small fresh rosemary sprigs

2 red onions

50g caster sugar

50ml red wine vinegar

2 fresh thyme sprigs

sea salt and freshly ground black pepper

crusty bread and green salad leaves, to serve

1 Preheat the oven to 200°C/400°F/Gas mark 6. Place the goat's cheeses on a baking tray, pierce with sprigs of rosemary and season with salt and pepper. Bake for 8–10 minutes, until soft and golden.

2 Meanwhile, slice the onions. Place the onions, sugar, vinegar and thyme in a pan, bring to the boil and let bubble until sticky, about 5–8 minutes.

3 Serve each goat's cheese with a spoonful of onion jam and some crusty bread and salad leaves.

HOT-AND-SOUR SOUP WITH CHILLI & SHIITAKE MUSHROOMS

Supermarkets sell great ready-made liquid stocks now, which help so much to add flavour. Once you master the base you can turn this into whatever you want. I love it with some pan-fried mackerel or leftover duck shredded into it. You could use fish or chicken stock, too, depending on what you want to put in it.

Serves 4

4 lemongrass stalks

1 bunch fresh coriander

1 litre vegetable stock

6 kaffir lime leaves

50g palm sugar

2 tbsp tamarind paste mixed with 40ml water

200g shiitake mushrooms

3 fresh red chillies

8 plum tomatoes

200g tofu

sea salt and freshly ground black pepper

1 Crush the lemongrass stalks and chop the coriander, reserving the stalks.

2 In a large saucepan, bring the vegetable stock, lemongrass, coriander stalks, lime leaves, palm sugar and tamarind mixture to the boil.

3 Thinly slice the mushrooms and chillies, and deseed and slice the tomatoes. Slice the tofu.

4 Divide the chillies, mushrooms, tomatoes and tofu among 4 serving bowls.

5 Strain the stock into a large jug and season with salt and pepper. Pour it over the vegetables and tofu and finish with the chopped coriander. Leave to stand for 1–2 minutes before serving.

SUMMER VEGETABLE VODKA TEMPURA WITH AÏOLI

We created this while working on a bar snack, and this is the result: vodka and tonic batter! You could use gin, too, and the alcohol helps crisp it a lot. Make sure the oil is good and hot, though. The aïoli is easy to make, but you could also use shop-bought mayonnaise and add some finely crushed garlic to it.

Serves 4
100g courgette
100g aubergine
1 red pepper
1 yellow pepper
1 large red onion
vegetable oil, for deep-frying
coriander cress, to serve (optional)

For the batter
200g strong plain flour
1 x 7g sachet fast-action yeast
25ml vodka
175ml tonic water
pinch of salt
pinch of sugar

For the aïoli
4 garlic cloves
1 tsp salt
2 egg yolks
squeeze of lemon juice
200ml vegetable oil

1 First, make the batter: whisk together all the ingredients in a large bowl until smooth.

2 Cut the vegetables into batons.

3 Make the aïoli. Crush the garlic with the salt. In a food processor, whizz together the egg yolks, garlic and lemon juice, then slowly drizzle in the vegetable oil until thick and emulsified. Set aside.

4 Heat the oil in a deep-fryer to 160°C/320°F. Dip the vegetables in the batter and deep fry for 2–3 minutes, until crisp and golden. Remove and drain on kitchen paper.

5 Season the vegetable tempura with salt and pepper, scatter with coriander cress, if using, and serve with the aïoli.

Serves 4

250g Ogleshield cheese
2 fresh rosemary sprigs
4 slices thick white bread
2 egg yolks
1 tbsp wholegrain mustard
1 tbsp Worcestershire sauce

1 Coarsely grate the cheese and finely chop the rosemary. Preheat the grill to medium.

2 Place the bread slices on a baking tray and toast them under the grill on one side until golden.

3 Meanwhile, mix the remaining ingredients together in a bowl. Spread the mixture over the untoasted side of the bread and return to the grill for 2–3 minutes, until golden and bubbling.

Ogleshield is made in Somerset by the same people who make the famous Montgomery's Cheddar, but it's made with Jersey cow's milk instead. They only produce a small amount, mainly because they have a small herd, but it's worth looking out for, as the flavour is fantastic. You can substitute other strong-flavoured hard cheeses. We sometimes serve it as a bar snack in the restaurant, with home-made pickles and a small bottle of Worcestershire sauce on the side, and it goes down a treat.

OGLESHIELD TOASTS

SMOKED SALMON MOUSSE WITH MELBA TOAST

Melba toast may seem a bit dated, but there's no better accompaniment for a salmon mousse. To make it, all you need to do is toast the bread on both sides, cut the crusts off and slice in two horizontally, turn the untoasted side up and rub off the excess bread with your fingers, toast it again, and that's it. Don't leave the blender on for too long when you make the mousse, or the mixture may split.

Serves 4

1 tbsp fresh dill leaves

300g smoked salmon

100ml crème fraîche

50ml double cream

juice and grated zest of 1 lemon

4 slices sliced white bread

sea salt and freshly ground black pepper

lemon wedges, to serve

1 Roughly chop the dill. Place the salmon, dill, crème fraîche, double cream, lemon juice and zest in a food processor, season with salt and pepper and blitz until smooth. Divide among 4 individual serving dishes and chill.

2 To make the melba toast, remove the crusts, then slice the bread in half horizontally to make very thin slices. Toast and serve with the mousse and lemon wedges.

CRAB & SWEETCORN SPRING ROLLS WITH SWEET CHILLI DIPPING SAUCE

Is it just me, or is chilli sauce addictive? You can buy crab meat quite easily now, but you could also adapt it using salmon or prawns. This is an easy dish to prepare and everyone will love it.

Serves 4

2 spring onions

1 small bunch fresh coriander

200g white crab meat

200g sweetcorn, drained

4 large spring roll wrappers (or 16 small ones to make canapé-sized rolls)

vegetable oil, for deep-frying

sea salt and freshly ground black pepper

100ml sweet chilli dipping sauce, to serve

1 Finely slice the spring onions and chop the coriander. Mix together the spring onions, crab meat, sweetcorn and coriander, and season with salt and pepper.

2 Divide the mixture evenly between the spring roll wrappers and wet the edges with a pastry brush dipped in water. Fold in the outer edges in by 2cm, then roll up tightly.

3 Heat the oil in a deep-fryer to 160°C/320°F. Add the spring rolls in batches and cook for 2–3 minutes, or until golden brown. Remove and drain on kitchen paper.

4 Serve hot with the sweet chilli dipping sauce.

Serves 4

1 small bunch fresh coriander
75g brown crab meat
125g white crab meat
100g ready-made mashed potatoes
50g panko breadcrumbs
1 tbsp poppy seeds
1 tbsp sesame seeds
25g flour
1 egg, lightly beaten
vegetable oil, for frying
sea salt and freshly ground black pepper

For the chilli jam
2 fresh red chillies
75g caster sugar
juice of 4 limes

1 Chop the coriander and mix half of it with both types of crab meat and the mashed potatoes. Season with salt and pepper and shape into 4 rounds (you could also make little canapé-sized cakes if you prefer).

2 Mix together the panko breadcrumbs, poppy seeds and sesame seeds. Season the flour with salt and pepper. Lightly coat the crab cakes in the flour, dip them in the beaten egg, and then into the breadcrumb mixture.

3 Heat the oil in a large non-stick frying pan, add the crab cakes and cook over a medium heat for 2–3 minutes on each side.

4 While the crab cakes are cooking, chop the chillies. Put the sugar, chillies and lime juice in a small pan and heat gently. Once the sugar has dissolved, add the remaining chopped coriander, pour it into a dip pot and serve alongside the crab cakes.

Bought mashed potatoes are so good, and a really handy shortcut. I've seen how they're made in bulk in the factories – they use butter, and cream too! It's great as a binding ingredient for fish cakes, saving you so much time and stress. Chopped smoked salmon or any cooked fish would work here, but since it is already cooked, don't over-fry them. That way they won't break up in the pan.

CORIANDER CRAB CAKES WITH CHILLI JAM

AVOCADO & CRAB TIAN WITH CITRUS SALAD & DILL CRÈME FRAÎCHE

Crab meat has to be one of my favourite ingredients, and in its classic combination with avocado, it has been around on menus for as long as scampi and chips. Along with grapefruit, the three taste great together. This is a perfect quick starter for a dinner party.

Serves 4

2 ripe avocados
1 pink grapefruit
1 large orange
2 tbsp fresh dill leaves
100ml crème fraîche
400g white crab meat
sea salt and freshly ground black pepper

1 Peel and slice the avocados and segment the grapefruit and orange. To do this, cut the skin and pith off with a sharp knife, then cut into the fruit between the membranes to release the segments. Cut them into small pieces.

2 Finely chop the dill. Whisk together the crème fraîche and dill in a small bowl and season with salt and pepper.

3 Take 4 chef rings or large, deep cookie cutters. Place some avocado slices in the bottom of each one and top with crab meat. Finish with a layer of the dressing.

4 Slide a wide spatula or fish slice under each chef ring and carefully transfer it to a plate. Remove the chef ring and scatter the citrus fruit around it, and more dressing, if you like.

POTTED SHRIMPS

This is one of my all-time favourite things to eat. You can buy the shrimps ready peeled and make this dish very quickly. The secret is in the spicing: mace or cayenne pepper, or both, are vital, as is black pepper. I love it spread over warm toast, with the shrimp butter melting into it.

Serves 4

200g cooked brown shrimp, peeled

100g butter, softened

pinch of ground mace

pinch of cayenne pepper

1 tsp paprika

juice and grated zest of 1 lemon

4 thin slices white bread

sea salt and freshly ground black pepper

watercress leaves, to serve (optional)

1 Gently mix all the ingredients together in a bowl and season with salt and pepper.

2 Toast the bread and serve with the potted shrimp alongside, and a few watercress leaves, if you like.

Serves 4

2 egg yolks
50ml olive oil
25ml cider vinegar
25ml tomato ketchup
20ml brandy
pinch of cayenne pepper
4 little gem lettuces
300g cooked crayfish
sea salt and freshly ground black pepper
brown bread and butter, to serve
lemon wedges, to serve (optional)

1 Make the spicy mayonnaise: place the egg yolks in a small food processor and blitz while slowly drizzling in the oil, then the cider vinegar. Add the ketchup, brandy and cayenne pepper, and season with salt and pepper.

2 Quarter the little gem lettuces. If you like, you can chargrill them with a blowtorch for a few seconds, which gives them a caramelized flavour. Butter the bread.

3 Mix together the crayfish and spicy mayonnaise in a bowl. Place the lettuce on the serving plates, top with the crayfish cocktail and serve with the bread and butter and lemon wedges alongside.

Crayfish should be on the menu more often. You can buy them fresh, but they're often found peeled in tubs, ready to eat. The dressing is really simple, and adding cayenne and brandy gives it a great flavour. Home-made mayonnaise is easy to master after a few goes, and once you do there'll be no going back to the bought stuff.

CRAYFISH COCKTAIL WITH SPICY MAYONNAISE

PIRI-PIRI PRAWNS

Portuguese in origin, piri-piri sauce is becoming more and more popular, and since it works very well with any meat and fish, and can be made really quickly, it's definitely a handy one to know. The basis is the lemon and spices, and it often includes bay leaves, basil and oregano, but there are lots of different ways of making it.

Serves 4

4 garlic cloves

2 fresh red chillies

1 tbsp chilli flakes

juice and grated zest of
1 lemon

1 tbsp smoked paprika

50ml olive oil

20ml red wine vinegar

400g large raw prawns, peeled

1 tbsp fresh coriander leaves

sea salt and freshly
ground black pepper

crusty bread, to serve

1 First, make the piri-piri sauce. Chop the garlic and chillies and place in a small food processor with the chilli flakes, lemon zest and juice, smoked paprika, olive oil and vinegar. Blitz until smooth.

2 Pour the sauce over the prawns and season with salt and pepper. Heat a large non-stick frying pan, add the prawns and cook for 1–2 minutes on each side, until the prawns are pink.

3 While the prawns are cooking, chop the coriander. Sprinkle with coriander and serve with crusty bread.

DEEP-FRIED SQUID WITH PONZU

Flour and cornflour combined make a really quick crispy coating for squid. They need to be fried in very hot oil so that the squid doesn't toughen, and the cornflour crisps up. This is one of my favourites in the book for its quick, strong flavours – and it eats so well.

Serves 4

vegetable oil, for deep-frying
4 medium squid
25g self-raising flour
15g cornflour
2 tbsp fresh coriander leaves
2 tbsp fresh mint leaves
50ml olive oil
25ml ponzu juice
sea salt and freshly ground black pepper

1 Heat the vegetable oil in the deep-fryer to 160°C/320°F. Clean the squid, if needed, and cut it into rings. Mix the self-raising flour and cornflour together and season with salt and pepper. Chop the coriander and mint leaves.

2 When the oil is hot, toss the squid in the flour mixture and deep-fry in batches for 2–3 minutes, until golden and crispy, then remove with a slotted spoon and drain on kitchen paper.

3 While the squid is cooking, whisk together the olive oil, ponzu juice and chopped herbs and season with salt and pepper.

4 To serve, divide the squid among the plates and drizzle over the dressing.

Serves 4

2 Bramley apples

1 x 3cm piece fresh ginger

50g butter

4 thick slices black pudding
(about 100g)

25ml olive oil

8 large scallops, cleaned and
with roe removed

sea salt and freshly
ground black pepper

1 Peel, core and dice the apples and grate the ginger. Put them in a pan with 50ml water and half the butter and bring to the boil. Cook for 3–4 minutes until soft, then place in a small food processor and blitz until smooth. Set aside and keep warm.

2 Meanwhile, heat a frying pan until hot and cook the black pudding for 1–2 minutes on each side. Remove and keep warm.

3 Heat the oil in another frying pan, season the scallops with salt and pepper and cook for 1 minute on each side. Finish by adding the remaining butter, and once melted, spoon it over the scallops.

4 Place a spoonful of apple sauce on each plate, add 2 scallops and a slice of black pudding. Serve immediately.

This used to be on my restaurant's menu and the customers raved about it. We use Laverstoke Park Farm black pudding and hand-dived scallops. But it's the quick, easy ginger apple sauce that brings it all together, and it's one I brought back from my travels.

PAN-FRIED SCALLOPS WITH BLACK PUDDING & GINGER APPLE PURÉE

SCALLOPS WITH CAPER BERRIES & SAGE

The key to cooking scallops well is to use a hot non-stick pan with just a little oil, and not to turn the scallops until they have coloured. Add the butter when you turn them, and keep basting. It's only when you cook them this way that you'll realize how they're supposed to taste.

Serves 4

vegetable oil, for deep-frying

75g caper berries, rinsed and drained

1 small bunch fresh sage

25ml olive oil

12 large scallops, cleaned and with roe removed

50g butter

sea salt and freshly ground black pepper

lemon wedges, to serve

1 Heat the vegetable oil in a deep-fryer to 160°C/320°F. Add the caper berries and sage and fry for 1–2 minutes – they are ready when no more bubbles come off them. Remove and drain on kitchen paper.

2 Heat the olive oil in a large frying pan until hot. Season the scallops with salt and pepper and cook for 1–2 minutes, or until deep golden brown, then turn them over and repeat. Add the butter to the pan and spoon it over the scallops.

3 Serve the scallops immediately, sprinkled with the deep-fried caper berries and sage, with lemon wedges on the side.

1 piece stem ginger, plus 25ml
stem ginger syrup
2 garlic cloves
4 spring onions
25ml vegetable oil
400g raw tiger prawns, peeled
25ml soy sauce
sea salt and freshly
ground black pepper

1 Finely chop the stem ginger and crush the garlic. Slice the spring onions.

2 Heat the oil in a large frying pan, add the chopped ginger, spring onions and garlic and cook for 1 minute.

3 Add the prawns and cook for 2 minutes, or until they turn pink, then add the ginger syrup and soy sauce. Season with salt and pepper and serve.

This dish uses that amazing syrup in the stem ginger jar that we normally throw away – but don't get rid of it, because it tastes great and makes a wonderful dressing with dark soy sauce. It would work with most types of fish, and chicken too, so you can adapt the recipe to suit.

SAUTÉED PRAWNS WITH STEM GINGER & SOY

Serves 4

2 shallots

300ml fish stock

25ml olive oil

400g raw shell-on prawns

20g tomato purée

25ml brandy

100ml white wine

*50ml anise liqueur,
such as Pernod*

200ml double cream

80ml garlic mayonnaise

*sea salt and freshly
ground black pepper*

1 Dice the shallots and heat the fish stock in a pan.

2 Heat the oil in a large non-stick frying pan. Add the shallots and prawns and cook for a few minutes, until the prawns turn pink. Add the tomato purée, brandy, white wine and anise liqueur. Cover with the hot fish stock and bring to the boil.

3 Transfer to a liquidizer, blitz and pour through a fine sieve into a clean pan. Whisk in the double cream, season with salt and pepper and warm through, without allowing it to boil.

4 Divide among the serving bowls and serve with garlic mayonnaise.

My good friend Pierre Koffmann is a cooking legend, and he makes a mean fish soup. The secret is to use pieces of fish and not just the bones or shells, as is so often the case, which gives it a much better flavour. Here, though, we're using good-quality shop-bought fish stock. As well as aïoli or garlic mayonnaise, the classic garnishes are croutons and grated Gruyère cheese. Add them too if you want to feel as though you're in Marseille!

TEN-MINUTE FISH SOUP

BAKED HENS' EGGS WITH SMOKED SALMON & CHIVES

Dishes 'en cocotte' are found in many a French brasserie; they're quick and simple to make, and must be served straight from the oven. You could vary it by adding different herbs, using ham instead of salmon, or even adding a splash of cream.

Serves 4
40g soft butter
400g sliced smoked salmon
8 eggs
1 small bunch fresh chives
25ml olive oil
10ml white wine vinegar
80g rocket leaves (optional)
sea salt and freshly ground black pepper

1 Preheat the oven to 150°C/300°F/Gas mark 2 and grease 4 individual ovenproof dishes or ramekins with butter.

2 Place some salmon slices in the bottom of each dish. Carefully crack 2 eggs into each one and season with salt and pepper. Bake in the oven for 15 minutes, until just set.

3 Meanwhile, chop the chives. Whisk together the oil and vinegar and season with salt and pepper. Add the chives, reserving a few, and coat the rocket, if using, with the dressing.

4 Scatter the remaining chives over the eggs and serve with the rocket alongside.

1 Toast the crumpets and spread with half the butter. Set aside and keep warm.

2 Meanwhile, tear the salmon into strips. Chop the chives. Whisk the eggs and cream lightly in a bowl and season with salt and pepper.

3 Gently melt the remaining butter in a large frying pan over a medium heat and stir in the eggs with a spatula. Cook for no more than 2 minutes, stirring gently, until lightly set.

4 Top the eggs with the chives and serve with the salmon and warm crumpets.

Serves 4
8 large crumpets
50g butter
200g smoked salmon
a few fresh chives
8 eggs
50ml double cream
sea salt and freshly ground black pepper

I've tasted plenty of scrambled eggs in my time while judging the omelette challenge on Saturday Kitchen, but this is how I wish I could eat them. Toasted crumpets must be a northern thing – I was brought up on them, and my mother still loves them. They should be warm, with lots of butter. Come to think of it, maybe I should blame her for my love of butter!

CREAMY SCRAMBLED EGGS WITH SMOKED SALMON & BUTTERED CRUMPETS

SMOKED SALMON & CRÈME FRAÎCHE TART

This looks very impressive considering that you don't really make anything, and it's great for dinner parties. Buy the best-quality puff pastry, made with butter rather than margarine, and make sure the pastry is cooked through. Under-cooked puff isn't the nicest thing in the world.

Serves 4

soft butter, for greasing
1 packet ready-rolled puff pastry
1 small bunch fresh chives
300g smoked salmon
200ml crème fraîche
1 small bunch rocket, watercress or herb cress
sea salt and freshly ground black pepper

1 Preheat the oven to 200°C/400°F/Gas mark 6 and lightly grease a baking sheet. Cut the puff pastry into 4 circles, 5mm thick and 15cm across.

2 Place the circles on the baking sheet, prick all over with a fork and bake for 10 minutes, until golden brown. Leave to cool.

3 While the pastry cooks and cools, chop the chives and tear the salmon into large strips. Mix the crème fraîche with the chives and season with salt and pepper.

4 Push the top layer of the pastry circles down in the middle, leaving a 3cm border around the edge. Divide the salmon between the hollows in the pastry circles.

5 Drizzle the crème fraîche dressing over the salmon and sprinkle with the rocket, watercress or herb cress. If you like, you can return the tart to the oven for a few minutes to warm through before serving, in which case serve the leaves separately.

PAN-ROASTED CHILLI SALMON WITH CUCUMBER RIBBONS

I grow masses of cucumbers in the greenhouse and never really know what to do with them all. This is a quick idea I had that makes a great-tasting dish using dill, which is classic with cucumber. I wouldn't use the seedy part for this, as it's too watery. You could try it with chicken, too.

Serves 4
50ml olive oil
4 x 200g salmon fillets
100ml chilli sauce
1 cucumber
1 small bunch fresh dill
juice and grated zest of 1 lemon
50ml olive oil
sea salt and freshly ground black pepper

1 Heat the oil a large non-stick frying pan, add the salmon and cook for 2 minutes. Turn the salmon over and pour the chilli sauce over it, basting the salmon frequently with the sauce. Cook for a further 2 minutes, then remove and set aside.

2 Meanwhile, make the salad. Cut the cucumber into long ribbons using a vegetable peeler. Chop the dill. Whisk the lemon juice and zest, olive oil and dill together, season with salt and pepper and toss the cucumber in the dressing.

3 Flake the salmon into the cucumber salad and toss through gently. Serve immediately.

SUSHI SALMON WITH SIZZLING SESAME OIL & SOY

I tried this for the first time at a street market in Singapore. I'm not a big fan of raw fish, but this splits the difference. It was just one old boy serving about 30 people, but this was so simple, and the flavours so crisp, that I loved it. Yuzu juice, which you can buy online, would also be ace with the soy and sesame.

Serves 4
300g baby pak choi
25g white sesame seeds
2 spring onions
400g very fresh salmon fillet, skinless
75ml sesame oil
50ml soy sauce
1 handful beansprouts, to serve (optional)

1 Cut the pak choi into quarters. Bring a pan of water to the boil and steam for 1–2 minutes. Drain well.

2 Toast the sesame seeds lightly in a dry pan over a medium heat. Slice the spring onions.

3 Thinly slice the salmon and arrange it on the plates with the pak choi. Heat the sesame oil in a small pan until hot, then pour it over the salmon. Top with the soy sauce, beansprouts, if using, sliced spring onions and toasted sesame seeds.

Serves 4

1 bunch spring onions

1 fresh red chilli

400g salmon fillet, skinless

25ml sesame oil

50ml soy sauce, plus extra
for dipping

24 wonton wrappers

sea salt and freshly
ground black pepper

1 Chop the spring onions and chilli and cut the salmon into chunks.

2 Place them in a food processor along with the sesame oil and soy sauce. Season with salt and pepper and blitz briefly to make a coarse mixture.

3 Place the wonton wrappers on a clean work surface and place a spoonful of the mixture in the centre of each one.

4 Bring a pan of water to the boil and set a steamer over it. Brush the edges of the wonton wrappers with water and pinch them together to seal like a money bag.

5 Steam the dumplings for 2–3 minutes, then serve immediately with soy sauce to dip.

Wonton wrappers can be found online or in Chinese supermarkets. They come in large packs, but freeze well. Salmon is great for this, as it holds together well when steaming, but chicken and prawns would both work too.

STEAMED SALMON DUMPLINGS WITH SOY

PAN-ROASTED POTATOES WITH ANCHOVY & TOMATO

I first cooked this in Crete, mainly because they love their olive oil and fish over there. Some good dishes come out of true adversity: it was 40°C, we had very little time and very few ingredients. But it worked so well that I put it on my restaurant's lunch menu for a while. Buy good-quality white preserved anchovies for this, or even try to find fresh ones. It won't work with the dark brown ones in oil. Sardines work well too.

Serves 4

4 large potatoes

6 large tomatoes

50ml olive oil

2 tins anchovies, drained

1 small bunch fresh basil

sea salt and freshly ground black pepper

1 Slice the potatoes and tomatoes thinly.

2 Heat the oil in a large frying pan and cover the whole of the bottom of the pan with the sliced potatoes. Season with salt and pepper and top with the tomatoes, then the anchovies. Cook for 6–8 minutes, until the potatoes are crispy and tender.

3 While the potatoes are cooking, tear the basil into pieces. Scatter the basil over the potatoes and serve.

100g Parmesan cheese,
finely grated

100g pecans

140g mixed leaves, such as
frisée, watercress and
baby spinach

50ml olive oil

25ml balsamic vinegar

100g crispy bacon slices

sea salt and freshly
ground black pepper

1 Preheat the oven to 200°C/400°F/Gas mark 6 and line a flat baking sheet with baking parchment.

2 Place 4 tablespoons of grated Parmesan in separate piles on the tray, well spaced out, and flatten them slightly. Cook in the oven for 2–3 minutes, until golden, then remove and leave to cool on the tray.

3 Meanwhile, toast the pecans in a dry frying pan. Toss the salad leaves with the olive oil and balsamic vinegar, pecans and crispy bacon slices and season with salt and pepper.

4 Divide the leaves among the serving plates, top each one with a Parmesan crisp, and serve.

Pecans are one of those ingredients we haven't really seemed to take on board, but they're just as good in salads as they are in desserts. To vary this slightly, and make the pecans really nice and crisp, you could cook them in a sugar syrup for five minutes, then drain and deep-fry them before adding them to the salad.

CRISPY BACON & PECAN SALAD WITH PARMESAN CRISPS

600g chicken breasts
100ml Shaoxing rice wine
100ml sake
100ml mirin
100ml soy sauce
25ml sesame oil
50g caster sugar
vegetable oil, for cooking
2 bunches spring onions

1 Cut the chicken breast into 3cm cubes. Whisk together the rice wine, sake, mirin, soy sauce, sesame oil and sugar, and pour it over the chicken pieces.

2 Thread the chicken onto 8 skewers. Heat a griddle pan until hot, add the chicken and cook for 3–4 minutes on each side, basting well with the marinade until charred. Remove and set aside.

3 Meanwhile, toss the spring onions in a little vegetable oil and cook in the same griddle pan for 3–4 minutes, until charred. Serve the chicken skewers with the spring onions alongside.

This is one of the ultimate quick and simple foods, and it's a lot easier than people think. Keep basting the chicken while the sauce reduces and you'll end up with a lovely sticky glaze in the end. But don't reduce it too much or it will become bitter – the colour should be like a well-polished old table.

TERIYAKI SKEWERS WITH SPRING ONION

DEVILLED CHICKEN LIVERS ON TOAST

I love to serve this dish on thick toasted bread to soak up the sauce. It's so simple and so cheap; I've added a few mushrooms here, but you can do it just with chicken livers. Most liver is prepared for you these days, but it's important to remove any white or yellow bits before cooking. The essential part is not to overcook them, but to keep them nice and pink in the middle. That way you'll enjoy eating them so much more.

Serves 4

1 shallot

2 garlic cloves

25g butter

25ml olive oil

400g chicken livers, membranes removed

4 ciabatta slices

100g enoki mushrooms

50ml brandy

1 tbsp English mustard

½ tsp cayenne pepper

75ml double cream

1 tbsp fresh flat-leaf parsley

sea salt and freshly ground black pepper

1 Chop the shallot and crush the garlic. Heat the butter and oil in a large frying pan, add the chicken livers, shallot and garlic, and cook for 3–4 minutes.

2 Meanwhile, toast the ciabatta slices until golden and keep them warm.

3 Add the mushrooms and brandy to the livers, bring to the boil, then stir in the mustard and cayenne pepper. Season with salt and pepper and add the cream. Finely chop the parsley and sprinkle it on top.

4 Spoon the livers onto the toasts and serve immediately.

FAST

TUSCAN BEAN STEW WITH BASIL & PINE NUTS

We call it chef's chow: the tasty, quick food the chefs at the restaurant throw together for the team to eat before service, and this is a great example. You can use it as a base, too, by adding sliced chicken or fish along with the beans. It's nice to have some good olive oil and charred bread to serve with it. You can make your own croutons if you like, by frying torn pieces of bread in a little olive oil until brown and toasted.

Serves 4

1 large onion
4 garlic cloves
200g chestnut mushrooms
50ml olive oil
1 x 400g tin borlotti beans, drained
1 x 400g tin butter beans, drained
1 x 400g tin chopped tomatoes
25g tomato purée
100g pine nuts
1 large bunch fresh basil
200g ready-made croutons
sea salt and freshly ground black pepper
crusty bread, to serve

1 Dice the onion, crush the garlic and slice the mushrooms. Heat the oil in a large non-stick pan, add the onion, garlic and mushrooms and cook for 5 minutes, until softened.

2 Add the beans, tomatoes and tomato purée and simmer for 5 minutes. Season with salt and pepper.

3 Meanwhile, toast the pine nuts lightly over a medium heat in a dry frying pan, until golden.

4 Roughly chop the basil, then stir it into the stew.

5 Sprinkle the pine nuts and croutons over the stew and serve it with crusty bread.

1 Peel and coarsely grate the potatoes. Place them in a clean tea towel and firmly squeeze out all the excess liquid. Season with salt and pepper and shape into 4 equal patties.

2 Heat half the oil and butter in a large frying pan (or you can use individual pans if you have them), add the potatoes, press down well and fry for 2–3 minutes on each side, until golden brown.

3 Heat the remaining oil and butter in another frying pan and cook the eggs to your liking.

4 Serve a rosti on each plate with a fried egg on top, then add a dollop of crème fraîche and a good sprinkling of black pepper.

Serves 4

2 large waxy potatoes, preferably Vivaldi

50ml olive oil

25g butter

4 eggs

100ml crème fraîche

sea salt and freshly ground black pepper

Rostis have to be the perfect fast food. Sure, chips are in the mix as well, but these are served in my restaurant as a great lunchtime staple. Adding crème fraîche makes the whole thing less greasy. Remember to squeeze out the potatoes really well once you've grated them to make sure the mixture isn't too wet.

POTATO ROSTI WITH FRIED EGG & CRÈME FRAÎCHE

SINGAPORE CHILLI CRAB

Chilli crab has to be the ultimate street food for me. I was lucky enough to try it in Singapore, and it was one of the best dishes I've eaten. Most places have their own version of it, and it usually isn't served with much else, but you can mop up the sauce with some bread while you eat it. It needs to be cooked with the shells on, the idea being that you wear one apron to cook it and another one to eat it, as you'll get covered in sauce.

Serves 4

1 x 5cm piece fresh root ginger
3 red bird's-eye chillies
3 garlic cloves
1 tbsp vegetable oil
125ml passata
75ml sweet chilli sauce
75ml hoisin sauce
3 tbsp fish sauce
1 tbsp caster sugar
1kg cooked king crab claws
crusty bread, to serve

1 Grate the ginger, deseed and chop the chillies, and chop the garlic. Heat a wok until hot, then add the vegetable oil, ginger, garlic and chillies. Stir-fry for 2 minutes.

2 Whisk the passata, sweet chilli, hoisin and fish sauces together, then whisk in 75ml water and the sugar. Add to the wok and bring to the boil. Add the crab claws, then reduce the heat and simmer for 3–4 minutes, until the sauce has thickened slightly and the crab has heated through.

3 To serve, pile the crab on a plate and serve with plenty of crusty bread to mop up the juices.

3 garlic cloves

1 large onion

300g courgettes

4 tbsp fresh flat-leaf
parsley leaves

50ml olive oil

300g fresh egg linguine

750g fresh mussels, cleaned
(discard any that aren't closed)

150ml white wine

sea salt and freshly
ground black pepper

1 Finely chop the garlic and onion and thinly slice the courgettes. Chop the parsley. Heat the oil in a medium saucepan, add the onion and garlic and cook gently until softened.

2 Meanwhile, bring a large pan of salted water to the boil. Cook the linguine for 2–3 minutes, or until almost al dente (check the instructions on the packet and cook it for 1 minute less). Drain and set aside.

3 While the pasta is cooking, add the courgettes, mussels and white wine to the onion and garlic, cover with a lid and cook for 2 minutes. Season with salt and pepper.

4 Stir the linguine into the pan with the mussels and cook, covered, for 1 more minute. Check that all the mussels have opened; discard any that haven't. Sprinkle with the chopped parsley and serve immediately.

Mussels are one of the best types of seafood for fast cooking. The preparation is simple – just wash them in cold water and make sure any little tufts on each mussel have been removed (pull them off with your fingers if not). Fresh egg linguine cooks more quickly than dried, and tastes nicer too, but dried is fine: just check the packet for the cooking time. The secret with this is not to serve it too dry, so don't drain the pasta too thoroughly. You could also add some pesto from a jar if you like.

LINGUINE WITH MUSSELS & COURGETTES

2 lemongrass stalks
2 garlic cloves
3 kaffir lime leaves
500ml chicken stock
1 bunch fresh coriander
1 onion
2 fresh green chillies
50ml olive oil
200g Arborio rice
300g white crab meat
200g sweetcorn, drained
100g mascarpone
50g Parmesan cheese, grated
sea salt and freshly
ground black pepper

1 Crush the lemongrass and garlic and place them in a pan with the chicken stock and lime leaves. Chop the leaves off the coriander and reserve them, then add the roots to the stock pan. Bring to the boil, then strain into a clean pan and keep hot.

2 Meanwhile, finely chop the onion and chillies. Heat the oil in a large saucepan, add the onion and chillies and cook for 1–2 minutes, stirring.

3 Add the rice and cook for 1 minute, stirring. Keep adding the stock, a few ladles at a time and stirring well, over a medium heat.

4 Once all the stock has been added and the rice is al dente but still quite wet, stir in the crab, sweetcorn, mascarpone and Parmesan. Taste and season with salt and pepper.

5 Divide between 4 bowls and sprinkle with the reserved coriander leaves to serve.

People still think risotto is complicated, but really the key to it is the stock. You can buy very good fresh stocks now from supermarkets, which make dishes like this very easy to prepare. Like using sweetcorn from a tin, it shows you don't have to sweat over the stove to create restaurant-quality dishes.

CRAB & SWEETCORN RISOTTO

TERIYAKI SQUID WITH BEANSPROUT & RED ONION SALAD

Many people are still a bit unsure about squid, but we serve it a lot in the restaurant, and it's so quick, tasty and simple to cook that it's really worth trying. Most of the work involved in a dish like this comes before you start; it's all last-minute cooking and serving, which is the best way to do fast food.

Serves 4

300g white rice

1 tsp sea salt

1 small bunch fresh coriander

1 large red onion

2 fresh red chillies

1 x 300g bag beansprouts

25ml sesame oil

25ml soy sauce

4 large squid, cleaned

25ml vegetable oil

100ml teriyaki sauce

sea salt and freshly ground black pepper

1 Put the rice and salt in a pan with 500ml cold water. Bring to the boil, then reduce the heat and simmer for 12 minutes, until tender. Set aside and keep warm.

2 Meanwhile, chop the coriander. Slice the red onion and chillies. Mix together the beansprouts, onion, coriander and chillies, stir in the sesame oil and soy sauce, and season with salt and pepper.

3 Slice the squid into rings. Heat a wok until hot, then add the vegetable oil and stir-fry the squid for 2 minutes. Add the teriyaki sauce and bring to the boil, then season with salt and pepper.

4 Serve immediately with the beansprout salad and rice.

PAN-FRIED BRILL WITH SAUCE ALBERT

Every year I work with the Roux family on their fantastic scholarship programme, which trains young chefs in the traditional recipes. Sauce Albert is one of the classic sauces that has been adapted over the years; it was originally served with meat and was made from béchamel sauce with added vinegar, horseradish and mustard. However you make it, it's a classic that's perfect for home cooking as well as for chefs. I first learned how to make it in French restaurant kitchens at the age of twelve, and since then it's become a firm favourite for quick dishes.

Serves 4

50ml olive oil
50g butter
4 x 200g brill fillets
300g sugar snap peas
300g ready-made mashed potatoes
sea salt and freshly ground black pepper

For the sauce

2 shallots
25g butter
50ml white wine
125ml double cream
2 tbsp horseradish sauce
juice of 1 lemon

1 First, make the sauce. Dice the shallots finely. Melt the butter in a saucepan, add the shallots and cook gently for 2 minutes. Add the wine and bring to the boil, then turn down to a simmer and add the double cream and horseradish. Set aside.

2 Heat the oil and half the butter in a large frying pan, season the fish with salt and pepper and cook for 2–3 minutes on each side. Set aside and keep warm.

3 Bring a small pan of salted water to the boil and cook the sugar snap peas for 1–2 minutes, then drain.

4 Meanwhile, warm the mashed potatoes gently in a pan with the remaining butter for 2–3 minutes, until heated through.

5 Season the sauce with salt and pepper and add a little lemon juice to taste. Spoon the sauce over the fish, and serve the sugar snap peas and mashed potatoes alongside.

1 Halve the new potatoes, if large. Bring a pan of salted water to the boil, add the potatoes and cook for 12–15 minutes, until tender. Drain and keep warm.

2 While the potatoes are cooking, cut the caper berries into quarters and remove any stalks. Finely chop the gherkins and chives. Bring a pan of water to the boil for steaming the asparagus.

Serves 4
300g new potatoes
100g caper berries
100g gherkins
1 small bunch fresh chives
25ml olive oil
4 x 150g line-caught cod steaks
25g butter
300g asparagus
juice of 2 lemons
sea salt and freshly
ground black pepper

3 Heat the oil in a large frying pan, season the cod with salt and pepper and cook, skin-side down, for 2–3 minutes. Turn it over, add the butter and cook for another 2–3 minutes. Transfer the fish to a warmed plate to keep warm.

4 Meanwhile, steam the asparagus for 2–3 minutes, or until tender.

5 Add the caper berries, gherkins, lemon juice and chives to the pan you cooked the fish in, and season with salt and pepper.

6 To serve, divide the fish between each plate, spoon over the sauce and serve with the asparagus and potatoes.

Capers, gherkins and beurre noisette, or brown butter, are the foundations of sauce Grenoble. It goes with all kinds of white fish, the classic being skate wings, but those aren't the easiest to get hold of. I often do it with sole and crab, and you could try it with them too. Either way, it's all about simple, fresh flavours that go so well together.

COD WITH SAUCE GRENOBLE

SMOKED HADDOCK & HERB FISH CAKES WITH QUICK HOLLANDAISE

Yes, bought mashed potatoes. They're a great shortcut for binding the fish, and make this so quick, with no need to boil or peel potatoes. You could also buy the hollandaise to make it even easier, but this method is really simple, and making it yourself will mean it tastes so much nicer. If I told you to buy everything, it wouldn't be cooking, would it?

Serves 4

For the fish cakes

300g undyed smoked haddock

1 small bunch fresh chives

200g ready-made mashed potatoes

25g plain flour

50ml vegetable oil

sea salt and freshly ground black pepper

green salad leaves, to serve (optional)

For the hollandaise

4 egg yolks

200ml melted clarified butter

4 tsp lemon juice

4 tsp white wine vinegar

1 Cut the smoked haddock into small dice. Finely chop the chives.

2 In a bowl, gently fold together the smoked haddock, mashed potato and chives and season with salt and pepper. Shape into 4 rounds and dust with flour.

3 Heat the oil over a medium-low heat in a large, deep frying pan and cook for 3–4 minutes on each side.

4 While the fish cakes are cooking, place the egg yolks in a food processor and drizzle in the butter slowly so that the sauce thickens. Finish with the lemon juice and vinegar and season with salt and pepper. Serve immediately with the fish cakes, with some salad leaves alongside, if you like.

Serves 1

100ml milk

3 fresh or dried thyme sprigs

100g undyed smoked haddock, skinless

25g butter

15g plain flour

3 eggs

sea salt and freshly ground black pepper

green salad leaves, to serve

1 Bring the milk to the boil in a shallow pan with the thyme, then turn down to a simmer. Add the haddock and poach for 3 minutes. Remove the fish and keep warm. Reserve the milk.

2 In another pan, melt 15g of the butter, add the flour and cook for 1 minute. Whisk in the milk from poaching the fish to make a smooth sauce. Flake in the haddock and keep warm.

3 To make the omelette, beat together the eggs and season with salt and pepper. Melt the remaining butter in a frying pan and add the eggs. Cook for 1–2 minutes, stirring with a fork, then pour the fish filling into the middle of the omelette on one side. Flip the other half of the omelette over it and cook until just set.

4 Serve immediately with a green salad on the side.

I've tasted enough omelettes to know a good one when I see it, and this is one of the most classic recipes of all. It's often called Arnold Bennett after the man it was created for. He had good taste! It's easy to make, but you must use good-quality eggs and fish, and the haddock must be naturally smoked, not the dyed stuff.

SMOKED HADDOCK OMELETTE

PLAICE WITH SPICED SHRIMP BUTTER & LEMON FLOWERS

Before you go on a wild goose chase to the shops looking for lemon flowers, this is how they're made: cut the ends off a lemon, then peel it with a spoon, keeping it whole and in a round shape. Carefully trim off any pith, then slice it horizontally and you'll get slices shaped like flowers. Lemon flowers used to be a classic garnish in top London hotels, and I've finally found out how to do them. The sauce here is a bit like potted shrimps, but a bit spicier – it really is delicious.

Serves 4

300g new potatoes

1 tbsp fresh flat-leaf parsley leaves

75g butter

1 lemon

25ml olive oil

4 x 175g plaice fillets

100g brown shrimps

1 tbsp Gentleman's Relish (anchovy paste)

1 pinch cayenne pepper

300g mangetout

sea salt and freshly ground black pepper

1 Halve the new potatoes, if large. Bring a pan of salted water to the boil, add the potatoes and cook for 12–15 minutes, until tender. Meanwhile, chop the parsley. Drain the potatoes and crush them with 25g of the butter and parsley. Season with salt and pepper and keep warm.

2 While the potatoes are cooking, make the lemon flowers as described above.

3 Heat the oil in a large frying pan and season the plaice with salt and pepper. Cook for 1–2 minutes, then turn them over. Add the butter, shrimps, Gentleman's Relish and cayenne pepper, then cook for a further 2 minutes. Remove and keep warm.

4 Bring a pan of salted water to the boil and add the mangetout. Cook for 1 minute, until just tender, then drain.

5 To serve, divide the fish among the plates, spoon over the shrimp butter and top with a lemon flower. Serve with the crushed potatoes and mangetout.

Serves 4

4 x 175g sea bass fillets
25g butter
25ml olive oil
75ml white wine
50g golden raisins
75ml double cream
400g baby spinach
*sea salt and freshly
ground black pepper*
crusty bread, to serve (optional)

1 Season the fish fillets with salt and pepper. Heat the butter and oil in a large frying pan, add the fish skin-side down and fry for 2 minutes. Turn them over and cook for 1–2 minutes, then transfer to a warmed plate to rest.

2 In the same pan, bring the wine to the boil, then reduce the heat and add the raisins and double cream. Season with salt and pepper.

3 Place a large saucepan over a medium-high heat, add the spinach and wilt for 1–2 minutes. Season with salt and pepper.

4 To serve, spoon some spinach into the centre of each plate, top with the fish and spoon some sauce around. Serve with crusty bread, if you like.

The sea bass in the supermarkets is mostly farmed nowadays, and thanks to that the costs are kept down. If you can buy line-caught, do try it, though – the flavour is amazing. It's often called the king of fish, as chefs love to cook it and eat it. It works with so many other flavours too.

PAN-FRIED SEA BASS WITH WHITE RAISINS & BABY SPINACH

SEA BASS IN A PAPER BAG WITH HERBS & LEMON

'En papillote' is what the French call it, and it sounds much better than fish in a bag, but that's basically what it is. Cooking fish this way makes dinner parties so easy, as you can do all the prep beforehand and just place it in the oven, then take it straight to the table with no fuss. You could serve it with a simple salad – green leaves or thinly sliced raw fennel with dill would be nice. Any fish, or prawns, can be cooked this way. Just make sure you add a dash of wine or water to keep it nice and moist, and perhaps a knob or two of butter.

Serves 4

1 small bunch fresh chives

3 tbsp fresh flat-leaf parsley leaves

4 x 175g sea bass fillets

juice of 2 lemons

100ml white wine

sea salt and freshly ground black pepper

green salad leaves, to serve

crusty bread, to serve

1 Preheat the oven to 200°C/400°F/Gas mark 6. Chop the chives and parsley.

2 Cut out 4 large squares of greaseproof paper. Season the fish with salt and pepper and place each fillet on a sheet of greaseproof paper on a baking tray.

3 Sprinkle over the herbs and lemon juice. Fold the edges over to form a parcel, leaving one corner open. Pour in the wine and seal the packet.

4 Cook in the oven for 8 minutes. Serve each person a paper parcel to open at the table, along with a green salad and some crusty bread.

SALMON WITH SORREL CREAM SAUCE

I grow sorrel in the garden, and you can sometimes find it in supermarkets too. The key is not to overcook it, or it will discolour and taste bitter. It's used in many dishes around the world, mainly in sauces and soups, and I've had it in salads in Vietnam and Portugal. It works really well with salmon here, and would work with any other oily fish too.

Serves 4

1 small celeriac
milk, to cover
75g butter
50ml olive oil
4 x 200g salmon fillets, skin on
1 shallot
1 bunch sorrel
75ml white wine
200ml fish stock
200ml double cream
zest and juice of 1 lemon
300g purple sprouting broccoli
sea salt and freshly ground black pepper

1 Peel and cut the celeriac into small dice. Place in a saucepan with the milk and 50g butter, bring to the boil and simmer for 10 minutes, until tender. Drain and mash, then season with salt and pepper. Set aside and keep warm.

2 While the celeriac is cooking, heat the oil and 25g butter in a large frying pan, add the salmon and cook for 3 minutes on each side. Transfer to a warmed plate and keep warm.

3 Meanwhile, chop the shallot and tear the sorrel into pieces. Once the salmon is cooked and removed from the pan, fry the shallot in the same pan for 1 minute, then add the wine. Bring to the boil, reduce the heat and add the fish stock and cream. Season with salt and pepper, then add the lemon juice and sorrel.

4 Bring a pan of water to the boil and steam the broccoli for 2 minutes. Toss the broccoli in the lemon zest and serve it with the salmon, mashed celeriac and sorrel sauce.

GRILLED SARDINES WITH BACON & TOMATO CHUTNEY

All oily fish needs to be eaten as fresh as possible, and sardines are no exception. You also need something to cut through the oiliness – rhubarb and gooseberries are classic accompaniments, but this chutney has the same effect and it's a lovely way to eat it.

Serves 4

100g bacon lardons

12 sardines, back bone removed and butterflied (ask the fishmonger to do this for you)

50ml olive oil

sea salt and freshly ground black pepper

green salad leaves, to serve (optional)

crusty bread, to serve (optional)

For the chutney

3 garlic cloves

4 courgettes

50g sunblush tomatoes

150g caster sugar

150ml white wine vinegar

2 tbsp caraway seeds

300ml tomato juice

50g capers

1 To make the chutney, crush the garlic and slice the courgettes. Chop the sunblush tomatoes. Place all the chutney ingredients in a large pan and bring to the boil, then reduce the heat and simmer for 8–10 minutes. Season with salt and pepper and set aside.

2 Meanwhile, preheat the grill to high. Fry the bacon lardons in a hot pan for 3–4 minutes, until crispy. Remove and set aside.

3 Drizzle the sardines with oil, season with salt and pepper and grill for 2–3 minutes on each side.

4 To serve, place 3 sardines on each plate, sprinkle over the crispy bacon, and place a spoonful of chutney alongside. Serve with a green salad and some crusty bread, if you like.

1 Bring a pan of salted water to the boil, add the potatoes and cook for 10–12 minutes, until tender. Drain well.

2 While the potatoes are cooking, chop the shallot. Place the shallot, wine and cream in a pan, bring to the boil and reduce by half.

Serves 4
200g small new potatoes
1 shallot
200ml white wine
100ml double cream
400g clams, cleaned
50g cold butter, cubed
1 lemon
50ml olive oil
4 x 100g pieces skinless smoked eel
200g baby spinach
sea salt and freshly ground black pepper

3 Meanwhile, cook the clams, covered, in 100ml water until they open. Discard any that remain closed. Strain the clam cooking juices into the cream sauce.

4 Remove the clams from their shells and add them to the cream sauce. Whisk in the butter, add a squeeze of lemon and keep warm. Taste and season with salt and pepper if needed.

5 Halve the potatoes. Heat the oil in a frying pan, add the potatoes and cook for 2–3 minutes, until golden brown. Add the eel and cook for 1–2 minutes on each side. Stir through the spinach until it just wilts. Season with salt and pepper.

6 To serve, divide the eel mixture among the serving plates and drizzle with the butter sauce.

I love smoked eel. It's not used as much as it should be, but it goes with so many things, from black pudding to foie gras. It makes a great main course with the potatoes and clams in this recipe; do try to use Jersey Royals when they're in season. Don't overcook the eel, just warm it through so that the flesh stays lovely and flaky.

SMOKED EEL WITH CLAMS, NEW POTATOES & BUTTER SAUCE

1 Halve the new potatoes, if large. Bring a pan of salted water to the boil, add the potatoes and cook for 12–15 minutes, until tender. Meanwhile, chop the chives. Drain the potatoes and crush them with the chives, then season with salt and pepper. Set aside and keep warm.

2 While the potatoes are cooking, toast the almonds in a dry pan over a medium heat until golden. Remove and set aside.

3 Bring a pan of salted water to the boil, add the green beans and cook for 3–4 minutes until just tender, then drain and keep warm.

4 Preheat the grill to high. Season the trout fillets with salt and pepper and place on a baking tray. Top each one with a small knob of butter and grill for 2–3 minutes. Remove and keep warm.

5 Heat a sauté pan over a high heat and add the remaining butter. Cook until nut brown, then remove from the heat.

6 To serve, place a trout fillet on each plate with the potatoes and green beans alongside, scatter with the almonds and pour over the brown butter.

Serves 4
300g new potatoes
1 small bunch fresh chives
100g flaked almonds
300g green beans
8 x 150g trout fillets
150g butter
sea salt and freshly ground black pepper

Trout, most of which is farmed, needs to be cooked simply. Classic accompaniments such as brown butter sauce are a perfect match. I love it with almonds and green beans, as it reminds me of a little café I go to in Paris. It's not a fancy restaurant, just a simple corner café that serves great food like this dish.

TROUT WITH GREEN BEANS, ALMONDS & BROWN BUTTER

DEEP-FRIED SKATE WITH PAPRIKA AÏOLI

I had to include this dish because my chefs love it. Skate can be hard to find, but it's often available in good supermarkets and at the fishmonger. When you do find it, keep this recipe in mind and you won't be sorry!

Serves 4

vegetable oil, for deep-frying
50g plain flour
4 skate wings
4 garlic cloves
50ml white wine
1 tsp smoked paprika
200ml mayonnaise
sea salt and freshly
ground black pepper
green salad leaves, to serve

1 Heat the oil in a deep-fryer to 160°C/320°F. Season the flour with salt and pepper. Coat the skate wings in the seasoned flour and fry for 4 minutes, until cooked through and golden on the outside. The flesh should come away easily from the bone once it's cooked. Remove and drain on kitchen paper.

2 Meanwhile, make the aïoli. Crush the garlic and heat it in a small pan with the white wine for 1 minute. Pour this mixture into a small food processor with the smoked paprika and mayonnaise. Season with salt and pepper and blitz until smooth.

3 Serve the skate with the aïoli and green salad leaves.

TURBOT WITH CHARRED LEEKS & RED WINE VINEGAR TARTARE DRESSING

Nathan Outlaw is a two-Michelin-starred fish chef from Cornwall, and he's taught me a thing or two about cooking fish over the years. You never stop learning! This sauce was something he showed me. Simple and fresh-tasting, it goes with any fish you want to serve it with. Turbot can on the pricey side, but cod or even salmon would be good substitutes.

Serves 4

300g new potatoes

50g butter

4 x 175g turbot steaks

25ml olive oil

200g baby leeks

25ml olive oil

sea salt and freshly ground black pepper

For the dressing

50g gherkins

1 small bunch fresh chives

1 small bunch fresh flat-leaf parsley

75ml red wine vinegar

50ml olive oil

25g capers

1 Halve the new potatoes, if large. Bring a pan of salted water to the boil, add the potatoes and cook for 12–15 minutes, until tender. Drain and crush with 25g butter. Season with salt and pepper and set aside.

2 While the potatoes are cooking, prepare the dressing. Finely chop the gherkins and herbs. Whisk the vinegar and oil together, add the capers, gherkins and herbs, and season with salt and pepper.

3 Heat the oil in a large frying pan. Season the fish with salt and pepper and cook for 2–3 minutes on one side. Turn it over, add the remaining butter and cook for a further 2 minutes. Remove and keep warm.

4 Heat a griddle pan over a high heat, toss the leeks in oil, season with salt and pepper and cook for 3–4 minutes, until charred.

5 To serve, divide the leeks and potatoes among the plates, top with the fish and drizzle the sauce around.

200g new potatoes
200g French beans
4 eggs
1 garlic clove
4 anchovy fillets
2 egg yolks
1 tbsp Dijon mustard
juice of 1 lemon
200ml olive oil
50g apricot jam
1 tsp cumin seeds
1 tsp ground coriander
25ml vegetable oil
4 x 100g tuna steaks
4 little gem lettuces
100g cherry tomatoes
50g pitted black olives
sea salt and freshly
ground black pepper

1 Halve the new potatoes, if large. Bring a pan of salted water to the boil, add the potatoes and cook for 12–15 minutes, until tender. Add the green beans to the pan for the last 3–4 minutes of cooking time. Drain and set aside.

2 At the same time, place the eggs in another pan, bring to the boil and cook for 5 minutes. Drain, shell and cut in half.

3 To make the dressing, crush the garlic. Place it in a small food processor along with the anchovies, egg yolks, mustard and lemon juice, and blitz until smooth. Slowly add the olive oil and season with salt and pepper.

4 Whisk together the apricot jam, cumin, coriander and vegetable oil, and coat the tuna with it. Heat a griddle pan over a high heat, add the tuna and cook for 1–2 minutes on each side.

5 While the tuna is cooking, quarter the little gem lettuce and halve the cherry tomatoes. Divide the cooked beans and potatoes, lettuce, tomatoes, olives and eggs among the plates. Top with tuna and drizzle the dressing over the top.

Making your own dressing is the key to any good salad, and this classic is no exception. In France it's sometimes just dressed with good olive oil, but this is my dressing recipe, which includes a jam-based marinade I picked up in Morocco that caramelizes the outside of the fish. The spices go with it really well.

TUNA NIÇOISE SALAD

SEARED TUNA WITH COCONUT CHILLI CHUTNEY & CABBAGE SALAD

The idea for this came from a dish I had on holiday in the Maldives. The fish was amazing and the dressing was so simple. It was so good that I had it every day for lunch. I sneaked into the kitchen before I left to grab the recipe, so here it is, and I hope you enjoy it too. You can use desiccated coconut, but fresh is best.

Serves 4

4 x 150g tuna steaks
1 tbsp vegetable oil
sea salt and freshly ground black pepper

For the coconut chilli chutney

1 tomato
2 fresh red chillies
½ fresh coconut (or 100g desiccated coconut)
2 garlic cloves
juice of ½ lime

For the salad

½ white cabbage
1 red onion
3 tbsp fresh coriander leaves
3 tbsp fresh mint leaves
1 tbsp fish sauce
1 tbsp white wine vinegar
1 tbsp palm sugar
2 tbsp coconut milk
juice of 2 limes

1 Make the coconut chilli chutney. Roughly chop the tomato and chillies. Grate the coconut, if using. Pound the garlic, red chillies, tomato, coconut and lime juice in a pestle and mortar to make a paste, or process in a food processor. Set aside.

2 For the salad, finely shred the white cabbage and red onion using a food processor or mandolin. Mix them together in a medium glass bowl. Roughly chop the coriander and mint.

3 Heat a griddle pan until hot. Rub the tuna with a little oil, then season with salt and pepper. Sear the tuna for 2–3 minutes on each side. Remove from the pan and set aside to rest.

4 Meanwhile, mix together the fish sauce, white wine vinegar, palm sugar, coconut milk and lime juice and pour over the cabbage and onion. Stir well, then add the herbs and mix until well combined.

5 To serve, slice the tuna and arrange it on a board or long plate, and pile some cabbage salad on top of it along the centre of the slices. Spoon the coconut chilli chutney on top.

1 tsp cumin seeds
1 tsp coriander seeds
110g apricot jam
1 tbsp soy sauce
4 x 200g fresh tuna steaks
sea salt and freshly
ground black pepper

For the salad

400g mixed Chinese leaves
75g mooli (daikon)
2 fresh red chillies
3 tbsp fresh mint leaves
3 tbsp fresh coriander leaves
juice of 1 lime
1 tbsp fish sauce
1 tbsp soy sauce
1 tbsp palm sugar

1 Lightly crush the cumin and coriander seeds. Whisk the apricot jam, soy sauce, coriander and cumin seeds together in a bowl with salt and pepper. Pour the mixture over the tuna and turn it over to ensure it is well coated in the marinade.

2 Make the salad. Roughly chop the Chinese leaves and finely slice the mooli and red chillies (you can cut long, thin strips of mooli with a vegetable peeler, if you lke). Place them in a bowl with the mint and coriander leaves and toss to combine. Whisk the lime juice, fish and soy sauces and palm sugar together, then drizzle over the salad.

3 Heat a griddle pan until hot. Place the tuna on the griddle and cook for 1 minute, then turn it through 90 degrees and cook for 1 more minute. Turn the fish over and cook for another 1–2 minutes (for rare; cook it for a little longer if you prefer it medium). Remove the tuna from the pan and set aside to rest for 1 minute.

4 To serve, carve the tuna into thick pieces. Pile the salad onto a serving plate and put the tuna pieces on top.

This sounds weird, I know, but it really works. You can use salmon too. The key is to colour the outside of the fish – in doing so you caramelize the flavours at the edges and get a really tasty dish that's perfect for quick cooking.

BLACKENED TUNA WITH SPICED APRICOT GLAZE

Serves 4

300g white rice (optional)

5g sea salt

2–3 fresh coriander sprigs

2 pieces stem ginger, plus 50ml ginger syrup

25g Dijon mustard

25ml olive oil

4 x 150g tuna steaks

For the red cabbage slaw

½ red cabbage

1 red onion

1 bunch fresh coriander

25ml olive oil

25ml balsamic vinegar

sea salt and freshly ground black pepper

1 If using, put the rice and salt into a pan with 500ml cold water. Bring to the boil, reduce the heat and simmer for 12 minutes, until tender. Chop the coriander. Drain the rice and stir through the coriander. Set aside and keep warm.

2 While the rice is cooking, make the slaw. Finely shred the red cabbage, using a food processor or mandolin if you have one. Finely chop the red onion and coriander and put them all together in a bowl. Stir in the olive oil and balsamic vinegar and season with salt and pepper. Toss well to combine.

3 Grate the stem ginger. Whisk together the ginger, syrup, mustard and olive oil and coat the tuna steaks in it. Season with salt and pepper.

4 Heat a griddle pan over a high heat and fry the tuna steaks for 1–2 minutes on each side for rare (or a little longer if you prefer it medium). Set aside to rest.

5 Serve the tuna with the cabbage slaw and rice.

To save even more time, you could use Asian-style pickled ginger in this. The most important thing is not to overcook the tuna. Salmon is great served the same way, or even chicken.

GINGER & MUSTARD GLAZED TUNA WITH RED CABBAGE SLAW

BLOW-TORCHED MACKEREL WITH BEETROOT & BLINIS

This is a great dish I learned from a good buddy of mine, chef Tom Kerridge at the Hand and Flowers in Marlow. Blow-torching food is not new, of course, but cooking the mackerel this way gives it a great barbecued flavour without all the mess, and it's so quick. The key to it is to get really fresh fish.

Serves 4

4 cooked beetroots

100g redcurrant jelly

50g Dijon mustard

1 shallot

50g butter

12 large ready-made blinis

4 mackerel fillets

sea salt and freshly ground black pepper

small bunch fresh chives, to serve (optional)

4 tbsp crème fraîche, to serve (optional)

1 Dice the beetroot. Warm the redcurrant jelly gently in a small pan, whisk in the mustard and stir in the beetroot, then remove from the heat.

2 Thinly slice the shallot and separate the slices into rings.

3 Melt the butter in a frying pan and heat the blinis for 1–2 minutes, until golden brown on both sides. Set aside and keep warm.

4 Season the mackerel with salt and pepper and remove any pin bones. Place on a heatproof tray and blow-torch the flesh side for 1–2 minutes.

5 Place a piece of fish on each plate. Divide the beetroot among the plates, and place the blinis on the side. For an extra-special finish, chop the chives and stir through the crème fraîche, then place a tablespoon on each plate.

CHICKEN & PRAWN PAD THAI

You might need a few more ingredients than usual to make this, but the end result is worth it. To me, it's the ultimate street food, and the keys to it are the lime and fish sauce.

Serves 4

200g cooked chicken
1 small onion
2 fresh red chillies
1 x 5cm piece fresh root ginger
200g rice noodles
25ml vegetable oil
200g cooked prawns
25ml fish sauce
25ml soy sauce
2 eggs, lightly beaten
1 small bunch fresh coriander
50g salted peanuts
juice and grated zest of 2 limes

1 Slice the chicken, dice the onion and chillies and grate the ginger.

2 Soak the rice noodles in boiling water for 2–3 minutes, then drain and set aside.

3 Heat the oil in a wok. Stir-fry the onion, chillies and ginger for 1 minute, then add the chicken, prawns and noodles. Cook for 2–3 minutes, until heated through.

4 Add the fish sauce, soy sauce and eggs, and cook for another 2 minutes. Meanwhile, roughly chop the coriander and peanuts.

5 Drizzle over the lime juice and zest, and sprinkle with the coriander and peanuts to serve.

1 Heat a frying pan until very hot and season the chicken with salt and pepper. Add the oil to the pan, then the chicken, and cook, skin-side down, for 5 minutes, until deep golden brown. Turn over and cook the other side for 5 minutes, then set aside in a warm place to rest.

4 chicken breasts, skin on

50ml olive oil

2 fennel bulbs

2 lemons

100ml crème fraîche

50ml cider vinegar

sea salt and freshly ground black pepper

crusty bread, to serve (optional)

green salad leaves, to serve (optional)

2 While the chicken is cooking, make the salad. Thinly slice the fennel, using a mandolin if you have one. Finely grate the zest of the lemons and segment them. To do this, cut the ends off the lemons, then cut off the skin and pith to reveal the flesh. Cut in between the membranes to release the segments.

3 Whisk together the crème fraîche, cider vinegar and lemon zest, and season with salt and pepper. Toss the fennel and lemon segments in the dressing.

4 Slice the chicken, place some fennel salad on each plate and top with sliced chicken. Serve with some crusty bread and green salad leaves, if you like.

My chefs eat this with a plate of chips. Don't ask me why, but they do. Fennel has a brilliant flavour, and you can eat this salad hot, warm or cold. It makes a great picnic dish too.

PAN-FRIED CHICKEN WITH LEMON & FENNEL SALAD

CHICKEN WITH CORIANDER YOGHURT CHUTNEY

I ate a dish similar to this in Crete, which is famous for its olives, olive oil and herbs. Wild herbs such as marjoram and oregano grow all over the place, even by the roadside. The dish I had was made with basil, marinated and then grilled on the barbecue, but this version is great and would work just as well under the grill or in the oven.

Serves 4

300g large potatoes

25ml vegetable oil, plus extra for frying

1 fresh red chilli

50ml honey

25ml soy sauce

juice and grated zest of 2 limes

4 chicken breasts, skin on

sea salt and freshly ground black pepper

For the chutney

250ml thick Greek yoghurt

3 pieces stem ginger

1 small bunch fresh coriander

25ml sweet chilli sauce

juice and grated zest of 1 lime

1 Peel and slice the potatoes into 3mm rounds. Heat a large frying pan, add a little oil and sauté the potatoes until tender and golden brown on both sides. Sprinkle with sea salt. Set aside and keep warm.

2 Meanwhile, finely chop the chilli. Whisk together the honey, soy, lime juice and zest, chilli and oil, season with salt and pepper and coat the chicken in the mixture.

3 Heat a large frying pan until hot, add the chicken skin-side down and cook for 4–5 minutes on each side, until golden brown and cooked through. Set aside to rest for a few minutes.

4 While the chicken and potatoes are cooking, grate the stem ginger (you need about 1 tablespoon grated) and chop the coriander. Whisk all the chutney ingredients together.

5 Slice the chicken into pieces. Serve the chicken and potatoes with a big spoonful of coriander yoghurt chutney.

Serves 4

2 large fennel bulbs

*1 tbsp fresh chives
or Thai basil*

50ml olive oil

50ml soy sauce

4 cooked chicken breasts

*sea salt and freshly
ground black pepper*

*crusty bread or toasted pitta
bread, to serve (optional)*

1 Trim the fennel bulbs and slice them very thinly, using a mandolin if you have one.

2 Finely chop the chives or Thai basil. Whisk together the oil and soy sauce and season with salt and pepper. Toss the shaved fennel with some of the dressing.

3 Cut the chicken into long strips. Cover the bottom of a large serving platter with the fennel, top with the chicken and drizzle over the remaining dressing. Serve with crusty bread or toasted pitta, if you like.

Fennel is still not used enough in my opinion. It's really good in salads, but it must be very thinly sliced. Investing in a Japanese mandolin is a good idea, but for heaven's sake watch your fingers! This dish is super-simple and takes no time to make.

CHICKEN WITH SOY &
SHAVED FENNEL

CHINESE LEMON CHICKEN

Usually, when you order lemon chicken in restaurants, you can have it breadcrumbed and deep-fried, or poached. But this is my way, which is very tasty, and above all quick to make. Don't make the sauce too sharp with lemon, though.

Serves 4

400g chicken breasts
vegetable oil, for deep-frying
3 tsp cornflour
1 egg white
2 fresh red chillies
3 garlic cloves
juice and grated zest of 3 lemons
100ml chicken stock
25g caster sugar
25ml soy sauce
25ml sherry vinegar
1 bunch spring onions
sea salt and freshly ground black pepper

1 Cut the chicken into long strips. Heat the oil in a deep-fryer to 160°C/320°F. Coat the strips in 2 teaspoons of the cornflour, then the egg white. Season with salt and pepper.

2 Fry the chicken strips in batches for 4–5 minutes, until crisp and golden. Remove and drain on kitchen paper.

3 Meanwhile, make the sauce. Finely chop the chillies and crush the garlic. Place the lemon juice and zest, chicken stock, sugar, soy sauce, vinegar, garlic and chillies in a saucepan and bring to the boil. Mix 1 teaspoon cornflour with 2 teaspoons water and whisk it into the sauce until it thickens.

4 Thinly slice the spring onions and sprinkle them over the chicken. Serve the chicken with the sauce.

THAI CHICKEN & CASHEW STIR-FRY WITH CHARRED LIMES

Stir-fries are one of the ultimate fast foods. The secret is not to add too much oil, and to use a neutral-flavoured one such as groundnut oil, as most of the others will burn at the very high cooking temperature. Charring the limes is a great, speedy way to impart more flavour when you squeeze them over the finished dish.

Serves 4

300g white rice
5g sea salt
4 chicken breasts
1 onion
1 green pepper
100g cashew nuts
25ml vegetable oil
5g Thai green curry paste
100g sugar snap peas
4 limes
sea salt and freshly ground black pepper

1 First, place the rice and salt in a pan with 500ml cold water. Bring to the boil, reduce the heat and simmer for 12 minutes, until tender. Remove from the heat and keep warm.

2 While the rice is cooking, cut the chicken into strips and slice the onion and green pepper. Toast the cashew nuts lightly in a dry frying pan until golden.

3 Heat the oil in a wok, season the chicken with salt and pepper, then stir-fry it for 3–4 minutes, until golden. Add the curry paste and all the vegetables, then add 50ml water and cook for 2–3 minutes, stirring frequently.

4 Meanwhile, cut the limes in half and heat a griddle pan. Cook the limes, cut-side down, in the hot pan for 2–3 minutes, until charred.

5 Sprinkle the cashew nuts over the stir-fry, and serve with the charred limes and rice.

SPICY CHICKEN WITH ORANGE & GREEN BEAN SALAD

José Pizarro is a Spanish chef who has several restaurants in London, and he taught me this dish. It's so simple, and can be cooked in minutes in the deep-fryer. The smoked paprika and sherry vinegar are the important elements, so don't change or scrimp on these – you get what you pay for! It's simple, high-quality ingredients that make things taste good.

Serves 4

vegetable oil, for deep-frying

16 chicken wings

4 garlic cloves

60ml olive oil

1 tsp chilli flakes

1 tsp pimentón (sweet smoked paprika)

15ml sherry vinegar

crusty bread, to serve (optional)

For the salad

200g green beans

200g yellow French beans (or use more green beans)

4 oranges

25ml olive oil

25ml white wine vinegar

sea salt and freshly ground black pepper

1 Heat the vegetable oil to 180°C/350°F. Deep-fry the chicken wings in batches for 8–10 minutes, until golden brown. Remove, drain on kitchen paper and keep warm.

2 To make the salad, put the beans in a large pan, cover with boiling water, bring to the boil and cook for 3–4 minutes, until just tender. Drain and refresh in iced water.

3 Meanwhile, segment the oranges. To do this, cut the ends off the oranges, then cut off the skin and pith to reveal the flesh. Cut in between the membranes to release the segments. In a bowl, combine the beans with the orange segments.

4 For the salad dressing, whisk together the olive oil and white wine vinegar in a bowl and season with salt and pepper. Toss the beans and oranges in the dressing.

5 Crush the garlic cloves. In a small saucepan, gently warm the olive oil, garlic and chilli flakes. Remove from the heat and whisk in the pimentón and sherry vinegar. Pour the warm dressing over the chicken wings and serve with the bean and orange salad, and some crusty bread, if you like.

THAI GREEN CHICKEN CURRY

You can use shop-bought green or red curry paste, but do use with caution, as some of them can be a bit radioactive in terms of heat. If yours is, you can chill it down with a bit of lime juice, or by adding potatoes or aubergines to soak it up a little. You could try using fish instead of chicken, which would make this even quicker to prepare.

Serves 4

300g white rice
5g sea salt
600g chicken breasts
400ml coconut milk
200g sugar snap peas
200g baby spinach
fresh coriander sprigs

For the paste

1 x 5cm piece fresh root ginger
3 garlic cloves
2 fresh green chillies
1 lemongrass stalk
50ml vegetable oil
3 kaffir lime leaves
1 small bunch fresh coriander (including stalks)
1 tbsp caster sugar
1 tbsp fish sauce

1 Put the rice and salt in a pan with 500ml cold water. Bring to the boil, then reduce the heat and simmer for 12 minutes, until tender. Set aside and keep warm.

2 Meanwhile, peel the ginger and garlic and roughly chop the green chillies and lemongrass. Place all the ingredients for the paste into a mini food processor and blitz until smooth.

3 Heat a large frying pan, add the paste and cook for 1–2 minutes. Cut the chicken into cubes.

4 Add the chicken and coconut milk to the pan, bring to a simmer and cook for 10 minutes.

5 Stir through the sugar snap peas, cook for a further 2 minutes, then add the spinach. Serve topped with coriander sprigs, with the white rice alongside.

STEAK WITH PEPPERCORN SAUCE

When I was a kid, my folks used to take us out to the Berni Inn and Steakhouse for steak, jacket potato and peas. The steak always came with a peppercorn sauce, which I loved then and still love now. Like most of these dishes, once you realize how easy it is to make, I hope you'll try doing it at home.

Serves 4

vegetable oil, for deep-frying
400g oven chips
4 x 200g sirloin steaks
50g butter
400g peas
sea salt and freshly ground black pepper

For the sauce

1 garlic clove
2 fresh thyme sprigs
1 tbsp crushed black peppercorns
50ml brandy
200ml beef stock
200ml double cream

1 Heat the oil in a deep-fryer to 180°C/350°F. Fry the oven chips for 2–3 minutes until crisp and golden, then remove and drain on kitchen paper. Sprinkle with sea salt. Set aside and keep warm.

2 Heat a large frying pan until hot, season the steaks with salt and pepper and fry for 2–3 minutes on each side. Add the butter for the last minute of cooking. Transfer to a warmed plate to rest.

3 To make the sauce, crush the garlic. In the same pan that the steaks were cooked in, fry the garlic for 30 seconds, then add the thyme, peppercorns and brandy. Standing well back, and keeping the lid handy, tip the pan to ignite the brandy. Alternatively, just let it bubble for 1–2 minutes to burn off the alcohol. Finish by adding the stock and cream.

4 Bring a pan of salted water to the boil, add the peas and cook for 1–2 minutes, then drain.

5 Place a steak on each place with the sauce poured over, and the chips and peas on the side.

STEAK FRITES WITH BÉARNAISE

Béarnaise sauce is chefs' food. For me, it's the best sauce to have with steak, and it's great for dunking chips in. I like the pieces of onion left in it, but they're often sieved out. Leave them in, and once they've combined with the tarragon, this has to be one of the best sauces around.

Serves 4

1 shallot
3 tbsp fresh tarragon leaves
25ml tarragon vinegar
50ml white wine
1 tsp white peppercorns
4 x 250g rump steaks
25ml olive oil
vegetable oil, for deep-frying
400g oven chips
200g butter
4 egg yolks
1 lemon (optional)
1 head chicory
2 little gem lettuces
50g rocket
sea salt and freshly ground black pepper

1 First, prepare the base for the béarnaise. Dice the shallot and chop the tarragon. Heat the vinegar, wine, peppercorns and shallot in a pan, then drain and cool.

2 Heat a large frying pan or griddle pan until hot, season the steaks with salt and pepper and drizzle with olive oil. Fry for 2–3 minutes on each side, then set aside in a warm place to rest.

3 While the steaks are cooking, heat the vegetable oil in a deep-fryer to 180°C/350°F. Fry the oven chips for 2–3 minutes until crisp and golden, then remove and drain on kitchen paper. Sprinkle with sea salt.

4 Meanwhile, finish the béarnaise. Melt the butter. In a small food processor, blitz the eggs with the vinegar mixture, then slowly add the butter. Pour into a bowl and stir in the chopped tarragon. Season with salt and pepper, and a little lemon if needed.

5 Slice the chicory, cut the little gem into quarters and mix them with the rocket leaves. Serve a steak on each plate, divide the salad and chips among them, and spoon over the béarnaise.

Serves 4

1 onion
200g button mushrooms
500g beef fillet
200g tagliatelle
125g butter
*1 small bunch fresh
flat-leaf parsley*
15g tomato purée
25g Dijon mustard
1 tsp smoked paprika
100ml beef stock
100ml brandy
200ml double cream
*sea salt and freshly
ground black pepper*

1 Peel and dice the onion, slice the mushrooms and cut the beef fillet into thin strips.

2 Bring a large pan of salted water to the boil and cook the tagliatelle for 8–10 minutes (check the instructions on the packet), until just al dente.

3 Heat a large saucepan and add 75g butter. When it foams, add the onion and mushrooms and cook gently for 2 minutes.

4 Add the beef and cook for 3 minutes. Meanwhile, chop the parsley.

5 Stir the tomato purée, Dijon mustard, smoked paprika, stock, brandy and cream into the beef. Bring to a simmer, season with salt and pepper and sprinkle with the parsley.

6 Drain the tagliatelle well, toss the remaining butter through it to melt, and serve with the beef.

There are a few classics in this book, but this is a real gem of a quick dish. It originally came from Moscow, and was made with beef pieces that were cooked slowly, but when cooking it the fast way, use fillet or sirloin, as this will give you the best result. It's traditional to use the tail end of the fillet, which cooks very quickly.

BEEF STROGANOFF

CHINESE CHILLI BEEF

The first time you cook this you won't believe how simple it is. The most important part is to deep-fry the beef strips well to get them really crispy. Then it's all about the sauce, and not adding the beef too early – you want the end result to be nice and sticky, but not soggy.

Serves 4

300g long-grain rice

1 tsp sea salt

4 tbsp Szechuan peppercorns

grated zest of 2 oranges

2 tbsp vegetable oil, plus extra for deep-frying

400g beef fillet

8 tbsp rice or potato flour, or cornflour

2 fresh red chillies

1 x 10cm piece fresh root ginger

150ml rice wine vinegar

150g caster sugar

4 tbsp soy sauce

2 tsp chilli flakes

1 small bunch fresh coriander

3 spring onions

1 Put the rice and salt in a pan with 500ml cold water. Bring to the boil, reduce the heat and simmer for 12 minutes, until tender. Set aside and keep warm.

2 While the rice is cooking, heat a frying pan until hot, add the Szechuan peppercorns and toast for 1 minute. Place in a pestle and mortar and crush thoroughly, then add the orange zest and crush again.

3 Heat the oil in a deep-fryer to 190°C/375°F. Cut the beef into strips and coat with the vegetable oil. Put the salt and flour into a bowl, add the Szechuan pepper mixture and mix well to combine. Add the beef and toss to coat each piece thoroughly. Cook the beef in batches for 2 minutes, until crispy, in the deep-fryer. Remove and drain on kitchen paper.

4 Make the sauce. Chop the chillies and grate the ginger. Heat a frying pan until hot, add the vinegar, sugar and soy sauce and bring to the boil. Add the chillies, chilli flakes and ginger and cook for a few minutes, until just thickened. Add the cooked beef to the sauce and cook for 1–2 minutes, tossing to make sure everything is coated.

5 Chop the coriander and slice the spring onions. Serve the beef with the rice and the coriander and spring onions sprinkled on top.

For the beef

400g beef fillet

3 garlic cloves

2 small round shallots

50ml coconut milk

50g crunchy peanut butter

2 tsp chilli oil

25ml rice wine vinegar

1 tbsp soy sauce

1 tsp caster sugar

juice and grated zest of 1 lime

25ml vegetable oil

sea salt and freshly
ground black pepper

For the salad

2 garlic cloves

1 x 5cm piece fresh root ginger

1 fresh long red chilli

3 tbsp fresh mint leaves

3 tbsp fresh coriander leaves

50g palm sugar

25ml rice wine vinegar

25ml lime juice

1 tbsp vegetable oil

4 little gem lettuces

1 Thinly slice the beef. Roughly chop the garlic cloves and shallots. Place all the ingredients except the vegetable oil and beef in a food processor and blitz to make a smooth purée. Season with salt and pepper, add the beef and stir until well combined.

2 Heat a griddle pan until hot, add the vegetable oil and beef and cook for 2–3 minutes on each side for medium-rare, or longer if you prefer. Remove and set aside to rest.

3 While the beef is cooking, make the Thai salad. Roughly chop the garlic, ginger, chilli and herbs. Pound them to a paste with the palm sugar in a pestle and mortar. Transfer the mixture to a bowl, add the rice wine vinegar, lime juice and oil and stir until well combined.

4 Separate the leaves of the little gem lettuce and toss them in the dressing. Slice the beef and arrange it on top of the salad, then serve.

The key to this recipe is the dressing, which works so well with salads. It's brilliant as a dressing with barbecued food, and gives a great fresh flavour to anything it's served with – whether it's with meat or fish, I love it. All the ingredients can be found easily in the supermarket; there's no substitute for palm sugar, which has a flavour all of its own.

WARM THAI BEEF SALAD WITH CHILLI, LIME & PALM SUGAR

1 Put the polenta in a pan with the hot stock, season with salt and pepper and cook gently for 5 minutes, stirring, until thick.

2 Meanwhile, heat a griddle pan until hot. Season the calves' liver with salt and pepper, drizzle with oil, then cook for 3–4 minutes on each side. Remove and set aside to rest.

3 Bring a pan of salted water to the boil, add the green beans and cook for 3–4 minutes, until just tender. Drain well and drizzle with a little olive oil.

4 In the same pan you cooked the liver in, fry the sage leaves for 1–2 minutes, until crispy. Remove and drain on kitchen paper.

5 To serve, divide the polenta among the serving plates, top with the liver and sprinkle over the sage leaves.

Serves 4
125g quick polenta
300ml chicken stock, hot
4 x 125g calves' livers
50ml olive oil
300g green beans
1 small bunch fresh sage
sea salt and freshly ground black pepper

I was brought up on a farm, so we used to eat most of the parts of the animals we looked after. Wednesday was liver, and I always used to go hungry. Now that I'm older I've realized what I missed out on when I was younger. So, sorry mum – after all these years I've started liking it. I still hate tripe though.

WET POLENTA WITH CALVES' LIVER & SAGE

VEAL MILANESE

People are starting to come around to eating veal again, thank goodness. In my opinion, British veal shouldn't be tarnished with the same brush as imported veal. Veal is a by-product from the milking process: we often have too many male calves, which are just disposed of. That seems crazy to me, especially as a farmer's son. Give it a try and I'm sure you'll love it.

Serves 4

300g Chantenay or other baby carrots (optional)
150g butter
25g caster sugar
4 x 200g veal steaks
50g plain flour
2 eggs, lightly beaten
100g panko breadcrumbs
400g baby spinach
sea salt and freshly ground black pepper

For the gremolata

1 garlic clove
2 lemons
2 tbsp fresh flat-leaf parsley leaves

1 Halve the carrots lengthways, if using. Place the carrots, 50g butter, the sugar and 200ml water in a pan. Bring to the boil, reduce the heat and simmer until they are tender and all the liquid has evaporated – about 10–12 minutes.

2 While the carrots are cooking, flatten the veal into 5mm thick steaks. Season each one with salt and pepper, then coat in flour, egg and breadcrumbs.

3 Melt 50g butter in a frying pan, add the veal and fry over a medium-low heat for 2–3 minutes on each side, until golden brown. Remove and set aside to keep warm.

4 Meanwhile, make the gremolata. Grate the garlic and lemon zest, finely chop the parsley and mix them together. Cut the lemons in half.

5 Melt the remaining butter in a large saucepan, add the spinach and cook for 1–2 minutes, until wilted. Season with salt and pepper.

6 To serve, place a piece of veal on each plate with some of the juices, add a spoonful of spinach and carrots, if using, and sprinkle with the gremolata. Serve with the lemon halves.

4 x 175g lamb fillets
200g couscous
1 small mixed bunch fresh
coriander, mint and
flat-leaf parsley
juice of 2 lemons
100ml olive oil
sea salt and freshly
ground black pepper

For the chermoula paste
2 red onions
1 small bunch fresh coriander
1 x 3cm piece fresh root ginger
100ml lemon juice
100ml olive oil
1 tbsp honey
1 tbsp ground cumin
1 tbsp paprika
1 tbsp turmeric

1 First, make the chermoula paste. Roughly chop the onions, coriander and ginger and place in a small food processor with the other ingredients. Blitz to a paste. Cover the lamb with the paste and set aside.

2 Pour boiling water over the couscous in a heatproof bowl until it is just covered, then cover with clingfilm and set aside for a few minutes until the water is absorbed.

3 Meanwhile, chop the herbs. Stir them into the couscous along with the lemon juice and 50ml oil. Season with salt and pepper.

4 Heat the remaining oil in a large frying pan, add the lamb and cook for 8 minutes, basting and turning frequently. Remove from the heat and leave to rest in a warm place for 5 minutes, then slice.

5 To serve, place a spoonful of couscous in the middle of each plate, top with the lamb and drizzle the chermoula meat juices around it.

I first tried chermoula in Morocco, but it's said to come originally from Tunisia. Either way, it's a great sauce with most meat or fish, so it's really versatile. The most important ingredients are garlic and coriander; the spices change, but cumin is nearly always included.

PAN-FRIED LAMB WITH CHERMOULA & HERB COUSCOUS

Serves 4

1 aubergine
4 courgettes
1 onion
1 garlic clove
1 green pepper
1 red pepper
12 lamb chops
50ml olive oil
1 x 400g tin chopped tomatoes
1 bunch fresh basil
300g ready-made mashed
potatoes
25g butter
sea salt and freshly
ground black pepper

1 Cut the aubergine and courgettes into dice. Finely chop the onion and garlic, and deseed and dice the peppers.

2 Preheat the grill to high. Season the lamb chops with salt and pepper and grill for 2–3 minutes on each side. Set aside to rest and keep warm.

3 While the lamb is cooking, heat the oil in a frying pan, add the onion and garlic and cook for 2 minutes. Add the remaining vegetables and the chopped tomatoes. Bring to the boil, reduce the heat and simmer for 5 minutes.

4 Tear the basil into pieces. Season the ratatouille with salt and pepper, then stir in the basil.

5 Meanwhile, warm the mashed potatoes gently in a pan with the butter for 2–3 minutes, until heated through.

6 To serve, place a large spoonful of mashed potatoes in the centre of each plate, put the lamb chops on top and a spoonful of ratatouille alongside.

Ratatouille is originally from Nice, which is why it includes such a colourful selection of vegetables and fresh herbs like basil, which grows all over Provence. Marjoram is sometimes used, or you can try mixed Provençal herbs. Some recipes roast the vegetables, but I like them simmered all together in a large pot.

GRILLED LAMB CHOPS WITH RATATOUILLE

GRILLED PORK CHOP WITH APPLE SCRUMPY MASH & BLACK PUDDING

I grew up on a pig farm, so I had to include a dish like this one! Choose good-quality, fat pork and cook it quickly under a hot grill. Doing this will make the fat crispy and nice to eat. The scrumpy added to the apples will really boost the flavour, and it's very tasty with the black pudding.

Serves 4

3 Bramley apples

75g butter

150g caster sugar

75ml scrumpy

300g ready-made mashed potatoes

vegetable oil, for deep-frying

100g walnut halves

4 large pork chops

50ml olive oil

200g black pudding

500g spring greens

sea salt and freshly ground black pepper

1 Peel, core and dice the apples. Place the apples, 50g butter, 50g sugar and the scrumpy in a small pan. Bring to the boil, reduce the heat and simmer for 5 minutes. Transfer to a food processor and blitz until smooth, or purée with a stick blender. Add to the mashed potatoes and heat gently for 2–3 minutes, until warmed through. Season with salt and pepper, set aside and keep warm.

2 Meanwhile, heat the vegetable oil in a deep-fryer to 180°C/350°F. Coat the walnuts in the remaining sugar dissolved in 100ml water and deep-fry for 1–2 minutes, then drain on kitchen paper. Preheat the grill to high.

3 Place the pork chops on a baking tray, drizzle with olive oil and season with salt and pepper. Grill for 4 minutes on each side. Slice the black pudding thickly and add it to the tray for the last 2 minutes, turning halfway through.

4 While the pork is cooking, shred the spring greens. Melt the remaining butter in a large pan, add the greens and stir-fry for 2–3 minutes, until just tender.

5 To serve, place some greens in the centre of each plate, top with the pork chop and black pudding, spoon some apple mash on the side and sprinkle with the walnuts.

PAN-FRIED CHORIZO & MERGUEZ COUSCOUS

Merguez is a type of spicy north African sausage, made mainly from lamb or mutton, but it sometimes includes beef. It's very popular in France, and it's sold all over the place there. It's heavily spiced with cumin, chilli or harissa, and sometimes has sumac, fennel and garlic added. It's often served with couscous like this, but trust me, you could serve it with chips and you'll love it all the same!

Serves 4

200g couscous
400ml chicken stock, hot
2 red peppers
1 Spanish onion
200g chorizo sausages
200g merguez sausages
50ml olive oil
1 large bunch fresh flat-leaf parsley
sea salt and freshly ground black pepper

1 Put the couscous into a large bowl, cover with the hot stock, then cover the bowl with clingfilm and leave to stand for 2–3 minutes.

2 Meanwhile, deseed and slice the red peppers and dice the onion. Slice the chorizo and merguez sausages.

3 Heat the oil in a large frying pan over a medium-high heat, add the peppers, onion and sausages and cook for 4–5 minutes, stirring, until sizzling and slightly softened.

4 Chop the parsley. Uncover the couscous, pour all the contents from the pan into it and stir in thoroughly. Add the parsley, season with salt and pepper, and serve.

BBQ BEANS WITH CHORIZO & WILTED SPRING GREENS

Chorizo comes in two types: one that you eat straight away, which is firmer in texture and slices easily, and one that's used for cooking, which is soft – that's the one you want here. I first had this dish at a restaurant in Ibiza, where most of the food is cooked on an open grill. It's a great way to use chorizo, and another good use for ready-made mashed potatoes.

Serves 4

400g cooking chorizo
2 onions
4 garlic cloves
1 x 400g tin kidney beans, drained
1 x 400g tin borlotti beans, drained
1 x 400g tin chopped tomatoes
100ml barbecue sauce
25g butter
400g ready-made mashed potatoes
400g spring greens
sea salt and freshly ground black pepper

1 Slice the chorizo and the onions. Crush the garlic.

2 Heat a large saucepan and fry the chorizo for 3 minutes, then add the onions and garlic and cook for another 1–2 minutes. Add the beans, tomatoes and barbecue sauce, season with salt and pepper, bring to a simmer and cook for 5 more minutes.

3 Meanwhile, melt the butter in another pan, add the mashed potatoes and heat gently for 2–3 minutes, until warmed through.

4 Bring a large pan of salted water to the boil and cook the greens for 2–3 minutes, until just tender. Drain well.

5 Serve the beans with the greens and mash.

Serves 4

200g pitted prunes

75ml Armagnac

600g pork tenderloin

300g green beans

300g ready-made
mashed potatoes

75g butter

150ml double cream

sea salt and freshly
ground black pepper

1 Chop the prunes and put them in a bowl with the Armagnac. Cut the pork into 1cm pieces.

2 Bring a pan salted of water to the boil, add the beans and cook for 3–4 minutes, until tender. Drain and keep warm. Gently warm the mashed potatoes for 2–3 minutes in a pan with 25g of the butter, until heated through. Set aside and keep warm.

3 Season the pork with salt and pepper. Melt the remaining butter in a large frying pan, add the pork and fry for 1–2 minutes on both sides, then remove and set aside.

4 In the same pan, add the prunes and Armagnac and allow to heat through over a gentle heat. Add the cream and season with salt and pepper. Return the pork to the sauce, stir through and serve with the mashed potatoes and beans.

This combination has been around for as long as snow, but it had to go in the book, just because it tastes so good. Pork fillet is great for fast cooking because it cooks very quickly, so don't keep it in the pan for too long. It has no fat on it and will dry out if overcooked.

PORK WITH ARMAGNAC & PRUNES

4 large duck breasts
50ml honey
25g white sesame seeds
50ml sesame oil
1 bunch spring onions
2 fresh red chillies
1 small bunch fresh coriander
300g pak choi
200g instant rice noodles
25g black sesame seeds
sea salt and freshly
ground black pepper

1 Preheat the oven to 200°C/400°F/Gas mark 6. Coat the duck in the honey, white sesame seeds and half the sesame oil. Season with salt and pepper.

2 Heat a large ovenproof frying pan and cook the duck for 2–3 minutes on each side, starting skin-side down. Transfer to the oven and cook for 5 minutes, then set aside to rest and keep warm.

3 Meanwhile, slice the spring onions and chillies, chop the coriander and quarter the pak choi. Cover the noodles in boiling water for 2 minutes, then drain well and stir in the chillies, spring onions and coriander.

4 Bring a pan of water to the boil and steam the pak choi for 2 minutes, until just tender, then drizzle over the remaining sesame oil and sprinkle with black sesame seeds.

5 Slice the duck and serve with the noodles and pak choi.

Most ducks in the supermarket are farmed, and, unlike wild ones, they can be cooked quickly, so they're great for fast cooking. My chefs and I were on a food tour of Ireland recently and came across a type of duck called Lissara from County Down. It was one of the best I've ever tasted.

SESAME-ROASTED DUCK WITH PAK CHOI & NOODLES

DUCK WITH UMEBOSHI & LOTUS ROOT

Umeboshi are a type of salted pickled plum. They're more like an apricot when raw, but can be found in shops in puréed form. Their sour flavour makes them perfect for fatty ingredients such duck and pork.

Serves 4

200g white rice

70g fresh root ginger

75ml honey

15g umeboshi paste

½ tsp Chinese five spice

4 large duck breasts

vegetable oil, for deep-frying

50g lotus root

8 spring onions

sea salt and freshly ground black pepper

1 Preheat the oven to 160°C/320°F/Gas mark 3. Put the rice in a large saucepan and cover with 400ml cold water. Bring to the boil, reduce the heat and simmer gently for 12 minutes, then set aside and keep warm.

2 Grate the ginger. Mix the honey, umeboshi paste, ginger and five spice, season with salt and pepper and stir well. Coat the duck in the marinade, reserving some for later.

3 Heat an ovenproof frying pan and cook the duck gently, skin-side down, for 3–4 minutes to render the fat. Turn it over and baste with the marinade, transfer to the oven and cook for a further 5–8 minutes. Remove and allow to rest.

4 Heat the oil to 160°C/320°F. Slice the lotus root thinly and deep-fry them in batches for 2–3 minutes, until crispy. Drain on kitchen paper.

5 Heat a non-stick frying pan and dry-fry the spring onions for 2–3 minutes.

6 Slice the duck and drizzle it with the reserved marinade. Sprinkle over the lotus root crisps and serve with the rice and spring onions.

1 Preheat the oven to 220°C/425°F/Gas mark 7. Using a pastry brush, grease 4 small dariole moulds with butter.

2 Break the chocolate into pieces. Put the chocolate and butter in a heatproof bowl set over a pan of barely simmering water and allow to melt gently. Remove and leave to cool slightly.

3 Whisk the eggs and sugar in a bowl for 10 seconds only.

4 Fold the chocolate mixture into the egg mixture, then fold in the flour, and divide between the prepared dariole moulds. Place on a baking sheet and bake for 8 minutes. Turn out and serve immediately.

Serves 4

*125g soft butter,
plus extra for greasing*

*125g dark chocolate,
70% cocoa solids*

4 eggs

100g caster sugar

60g plain flour

I call them three-star puddings because it's a recipe I learned while working in France at a Michelin three-star restaurant. It's easy and foolproof – the key to it, as with most chocolate puddings, is the quality of the chocolate. A dark chocolate with around 70% cocoa solids is best; too high a percentage and it becomes too bitter. They freeze very well, but they'll need an additional two minutes in the oven. Either way, be careful not to overcook them.

THREE-STAR CHOCOLATE PUDDINGS

BAKED CHOCOLATE & RASPBERRY MOUSSE

This is just what it says on the tin, really: a simple baked chocolate mousse, which could just go in the fridge to set before serving unbaked, if you like, but cooking it changes the flavour. Serve it with some pouring cream or ice cream, or both.

Serves 4

200g dark chocolate, 70% cocoa solids

25g butter

4 eggs

50g caster sugar

400g raspberries

pouring cream or ice cream, to serve

1 Preheat the oven to 200°C/400°F/Gas mark 6.

2 Break the chocolate into pieces. Melt the chocolate and butter together in a heatproof bowl set over a pan of barely simmering water. Remove and allow to cool slightly.

3 Meanwhile, separate the eggs, reserving the whites, then whisk the egg yolks into the chocolate mixture.

4 Whisk the egg whites with the sugar to form stiff peaks, then fold them into the chocolate mixture.

5 Place the raspberries in a large ovenproof dish measuring approximately 15 x 20 cm, then top with the chocolate mixture.

6 Bake in the oven for 12 minutes, then remove and serve immediately with cream or ice cream.

CHOCOLATE MOUSSE WITH MAPLE SYRUP & BANANAS

It's so simple, but mousse is still one of the desserts cooks can mess up. You won't go far wrong if you don't overwhip the cream, and don't let the chocolate get too cold or too hot. Put whatever you like in the bottom of the ramekins – adding a bit of rum would turn it into a real after-dinner treat.

Serves 4

2 bananas
4 tbsp maple syrup
200g dark chocolate, 70% cocoa solids
25g butter
150ml double cream
2 egg whites
50g white chocolate

1 Cut the bananas into small dice and place them in a bowl with the maple syrup. Stir well, then divide the bananas among 4 ramekins and set aside.

2 Break the chocolate into pieces. Put the chocolate and butter in a heatproof bowl set over a pan of barely simmering water. Allow to melt, then remove and leave to cool.

3 In separate bowls, whip the cream to very soft peaks and whisk the egg whites to stiff peaks. Gently fold the whipped cream and egg whites together, then fold through the cooled chocolate.

4 Divide the mixture among the 4 ramekins and grate the white chocolate over the top. Chill in the fridge, then serve.

1 Preheat the oven to 200°C/400°F/Gas mark 6. Cut the puff pastry into 12 rectangles measuring 10 x 5cm.

2 Place the puff pastry rectangles on baking sheets and prick them all over with a fork. Dust them with icing sugar, cover with baking parchment, put another baking sheet on top and bake for 10 minutes, until crisp and golden brown. Remove and allow to cool.

3 Meanwhile, place half the raspberries in a food processor and blitz them to make a smooth sauce.

4 Split the vanilla pod in half lengthways and scrape out the seeds. Whip the cream to stiff peaks with the vanilla seeds and transfer to a piping bag.

5 To assemble the millefeuilles, place a rectangle of pastry on each serving plate, pipe some of the cream over it, top with fresh raspberries and some of the sauce, then place another pastry rectangle on top and repeat. Each millefeuille should have 3 pastry layers. Serve immediately.

Serves 4
1 pack ready-rolled puff pastry
icing sugar, for dusting
400g raspberries
1 vanilla pod
400ml double cream

It used to be quite hard to make a good millefeuille without making your own puff pastry, but the ready-made puff is now very good when it's made with butter. Dusting it with icing sugar and baking it in a hot oven gives a nice, caramelized crust on every piece. You can do it under the grill, too, but make sure it doesn't burn.

RASPBERRY MILLEFEUILLES

BAKED ALASKA WITH HOT CHOCOLATE SAUCE

I went to America a while back, and managed to go to the restaurant that invented this dish to celebrate the US acquisition of Alaska. Why they made it out of ingredients from hot climates I'll never know, but it's traditional to use banana ice cream and serve it with an apricot sauce. Once you master the technique, though, you can make it out of whatever you like.

Serves 2

1 ready-made sponge flan base
400ml vanilla ice cream (or any other flavour)
4 egg whites
250g caster sugar
200g dark chocolate, 70% cocoa solids

1 Preheat the oven to 230°C/450°F/Gas mark 8. Cut the sponge into a 10cm circle and top with large scoops of ice cream shaped into a pile. Put it in the freezer until the meringue is ready.

2 To make the meringue, place a pan of water on the hob and bring to a gentle simmer. Place the egg whites and 200g of the sugar in the heatproof bowl of a stand mixer and place over the simmering water to warm the mixture, stirring the whites and sugar all the time.

3 After 5 minutes the sugar will have dissolved. At that point, place the bowl in the mixer and whisk the whites to stiff peaks – it should take about 5 minutes.

4 Place the meringue in a piping bag and pipe all over the ice cream and sponge, making sure there are no gaps. Bake in the oven until golden brown – about 2 minutes.

5 Meanwhile, make the chocolate sauce. Bring 100ml water and the remaining sugar to the boil in a pan. While they are heating, break the chocolate into a heatproof bowl. Pour the hot syrup over the chocolate and whisk until a smooth sauce forms. Serve with the baked Alaska.

ICE BOX CAKE

This is my favourite pudding in the book. I first tried it at the Magnolia Bakery in New York City (made famous by Sex and the City), and loved it so much I now make it at home. I hide the biscuit packet, though! The show's not really my thing (no cars or guns), but the cakes are great. The idea is that New York ladies are short on time, so they make this with a few ingredients, then put it in the ice box (in other words, the fridge) for a while to soften the biscuits into a cake texture – hence the name. I sometimes like to use soft fruit in the cream, but a coffee cream also works well with ginger biscuits.

Serves 10–14
400g raspberries (optional)
2 litres double cream
70 chocolate biscuits

1 Crush the raspberries, if using, through a sieve to make a smooth purée.

2 Whip the cream to loose, soft peaks and fold through the raspberry purée to create a marbled effect.

3 Place 7 biscuits in a circle formation on a cake stand, cover in a layer of the raspberry cream, making sure the biscuits are still visible at the sides. Top with another layer of biscuits.

4 Repeat the process until you have used up all the biscuits, and finish with a layer of cream. Serve immediately, or chill in the fridge for a few hours and serve very cold.

75g butter
100g soft brown sugar
125ml double cream
50ml whisky
50g marshmallows
400ml vanilla or
toffee ice cream

1 Place the butter, sugar and cream in a pan and heat gently until the sugar has dissolved. Add the whisky, then leave to cool slightly.

2 Put the marshmallows on a baking tray. Blow-torch them until golden and sizzling. Alternatively, grill them under a hot grill.

3 To assemble, put scoops of ice cream into individual dishes, drizzle over the whisky toffee sauce and top with the toasted marshmallows.

I always like to have a few bottles of whisky on hand for when my mates come over, and this is such a quick and simple way of combining it with one of the all-time favourite treats: ice cream. It's a great way to turn good-quality ice cream into a really special pudding.

ICE CREAM WITH WHISKY TOFFEE SAUCE & TOASTED MARSHMALLOWS

APPLE & MARZIPAN TART

Using ready-made marzipan and good puff pastry means this can be made in no time. Once you've added the apples you can freeze the tart, as they won't go brown. If you do, just make sure the oven is very hot so that the base cooks through.

Serves 6–8

3 dessert apples

75g butter, plus extra for greasing

flour, for dusting

230g ready-made puff pastry

1 tbsp icing sugar

100g white marzipan

75g caster sugar

100ml double cream

vanilla ice cream, to serve

1 Core and thinly slice the apples. Preheat the oven to 200°C/400°F/Gas mark 6. Lightly grease a baking sheet.

2 Lightly flour the work surface and roll out the puff pastry to make a large rectangle. Place the pastry on the baking sheet and prick it all over with a fork. Dust it with icing sugar.

3 Slice the marzipan thinly and spread it over the pastry base. Cover it with the apple slices and bake in the oven for 10–12 minutes, until golden brown and crisp around the edges.

4 Meanwhile, make the sauce. In a pan, melt the caster sugar, cream and butter together and simmer for 2–3 minutes, until golden.

5 Serve the tart with the sauce and vanilla ice cream.

QUICK STICKY TOFFEE PUDDINGS

Some chefs turn their noses up at cooking puddings in a microwave, but quick sponges like this can work really well – you just have to eat them as soon as they're ready, otherwise they don't taste as good. The brown sugar and treacle keep the sponge nice and dark when cooked. Many recipes don't include black treacle, but I think it adds a great depth of flavour to this classic dessert.

Serves 8

200g pitted dates
50g soft butter
175g dark muscovado sugar
30ml golden syrup
30ml black treacle
2 eggs, lightly beaten
200g self-raising flour
2 tsp bicarbonate of soda
vanilla ice cream
or cream, to serve

1 Pour 250ml boiling water over the dates and leave to soak for 1 minute. Butter 8 individual microwave-safe dishes or ramekins.

2 Transfer the date mixture to a small food processor and blitz until smooth, then set aside to cool a little.

3 Beat the butter, sugar, syrup and treacle together in a bowl. Add the eggs and the date mixture. Fold in the flour and bicarbonate of soda.

4 Divide the mixture among the prepared dishes and microwave on full power for 3 minutes.

5 Serve immediately with ice cream or cream.

1 Preheat the oven to 200°C/400°F/Gas mark 6.

2 Peel, core and dice the apples. Put them in a large pan with the sugar and cook for 6–8 minutes. Butter 8 individual dariole moulds or ovenproof ramekins.

3 While the apples are cooking, cut the crusts off the slices of bread and cut 8 of the slices into 3 equal rectangles. Cut circles from the other slices that are the same diameter as the moulds or ramekins. Dip all the slices in the melted butter and line the insides of the moulds with the bread rectangles, making sure there are no gaps.

4 Fill the moulds with the apple mixture and top with the circles of bread. Place on a baking sheet and bake in the oven for 10 minutes, until golden.

5 Whip the cream to soft peaks, if using. Let the charlottes cool slightly, then turn out and serve with cream or vanilla ice cream.

Serves 8

1kg Bramley apples
125g sugar
175g butter, melted, plus extra for greasing
12 slices white bread
double cream or vanilla ice cream, to serve

Apples, bread and butter: you can't really get any simpler than that, or tastier. Invented in the seventeenth century, this classic British pudding has stood the test of time since it was invented for Queen Charlotte, wife of George II. She was the patron of apple growers at the time.

APPLE CHARLOTTES

Serves 4
4 bananas
200ml double cream
200ml dulce de leche
300ml vanilla ice cream
4 scoops vanilla ice cream
4 chocolate flakes

1 Preheat a griddle pan until hot. Peel the bananas and cut in half. Grill them for 2–3 minutes until charred, then leave to cool slightly.

2 Whip the cream to soft peaks, then gently fold through the dulce de leche.

3 Place the bananas and ice cream scoops onto individual plates and top each one with a spoonful of cream and dulce de leche mixture.

4 Crumble over the chocolate flakes and serve immediately.

This idea came from a store in New York City, where they used to make it with leftover pieces of cake added to the mix. Then they froze it, and people came to buy it by the pot. I just had to try it, as it was one of the most popular things they sold. If you have any leftover cake, try doing the same.

BANOFFEE SUNDAE

BAKED BANANA & FILO PARCELS WITH PISTACHIOS

If there's one dish that's a bit fancy in here, it has to be this one. The team who helped me with the photo shoot laughed at me when I was making it. Timer in hand, they were convinced you couldn't do it in 20 minutes. Well, sorry guys, you owe me: 14 minutes and 32 seconds, cooked and done.

Serves 4

butter, for greasing
4 ripe bananas
100g shelled pistachios
4 sheets filo pastry
vanilla ice cream, to serve

1 Preheat the oven to 200°C/400°F/Gas mark 6 and lightly grease a baking tray.

2 Peel and halve the bananas lengthways. Toast the pistachios lightly in a dry pan, then chop them roughly.

3 Wrap each banana half with a scattering of pistachios in a piece of filo pastry (you'll need to keep half the pistachios for later). Fold over the ends to make neat parcels.

4 Place the banana parcels on the prepared tray and bake in the oven for 8–10 minutes.

5 Remove from the oven, sprinkle with the remaining pistachios and serve with a scoop of vanilla ice cream.

1 Blitz the biscuits in a food processor to make fine crumbs.

2 Split the vanilla pod in half lengthways and scrape out the seeds. Put them in a bowl with the cream cheese, crème fraîche and cream, and beat together. Swirl half the dulce de leche into the mixture.

Serves 4
4 digestive biscuits
1 vanilla pod
300g full-fat cream cheese
200ml crème fraîche
200ml double cream
200ml dulce de leche
50g butter
100g caster sugar
2 bananas

3 Sprinkle the biscuit crumbs onto 4 serving plates and top each one with a quenelle of the cheesecake mixture. Chill in the fridge.

4 While the cheesecake is chilling, put the butter and sugar in a frying pan and melt to make a caramel. Peel and halve the bananas and cook for 1–2 minutes in the caramel, until golden.

5 Place a piece of caramelized banana next to the cheesecake on each plate, and serve immediately.

This takes five minutes to make and even less time to eat. Who doesn't like these flavours? Shortly after the picture was taken, even I grabbed a plate of it. You can buy ready-made caramelized condensed milk now, as well as dulce de leche, from the supermarket, and this saves you so much time. The secret is not to make it too sweet. It will go better with the bananas if you don't.

FIVE-MINUTE BANOFFEE CHEESECAKES

BLUEBERRY, APPLE & MINT CRUMBLE WITH CORNFLAKE CRUMB

It might seem weird to put cornflakes in a crumble topping, something that only kids would do, rather than a chef! But this was one of the many things I picked up in America on my tour in search of the great and the good of the cake world.

Serves 4

2 large Bramley apples
50g butter
50g caster sugar
2 fresh mint sprigs
400g blueberries
pouring cream, to serve
(optional)

For the crumble

200g plain flour
100g butter
100g light brown sugar
100g cornflakes

1 Preheat the oven to 200°C/400°F/Gas mark 6.

2 Peel and dice the apples. In a saucepan, cook the apples with the butter and caster sugar over a medium-low heat for 5 minutes.

3 Meanwhile, finely chop the mint. Remove the apples from the heat and stir in the blueberries and mint. Transfer the mixture to 4 individual ovenproof ramekins.

4 Make the crumble. Place the flour, butter and light brown sugar in a bowl and rub in the butter until it resembles coarse breadcrumbs. Lightly crush the cornflakes and stir them into the crumble mixture. Sprinkle it over the top of the fruit.

5 Bake in the oven for 10 minutes, or until golden on top. Allow to cool slightly, then serve with cream if you like.

BLACK CHERRY CLAFOUTIS

This is basically a sweet Yorkshire pudding with fruit in it, but as so often happens, the French claim they made it first. So as not to upset them or the Yorkshire clan, here it is: my gran's Yorkshire pudding recipe, with fruit in it and cooked the French way. I still think we must lay claim to this one, though!

Serves 4

butter, for greasing
4 sheets filo pastry
400g cherries
2 eggs, lightly beaten
100ml double cream
75g caster sugar
100ml milk
50g plain flour
1 tbsp icing sugar

1 Preheat the oven to 220°C/425°F/Gas mark 7. Grease a 15 x 20cm rectangular ovenproof dish and layer the filo pastry sheets over the bottom of the dish. Allow the excess pastry to stand up around the edges.

2 Stone the cherries and sprinkle them over the filo pastry.

3 Whisk together the eggs, cream, sugar, milk and flour until you have a smooth batter with no lumps, then pour it over the cherries. Bake in the oven for 15–18 minutes, until golden and just set.

4 Allow to cool slightly, then dust with icing sugar to serve.

Serves 4

400g fresh or frozen
strawberries
50g caster sugar
½ tsp vanilla extract
150ml buttermilk

1 If using fresh strawberries, hull them and cut them in half. Line a baking sheet with clingfilm and spread the strawberries out on the tray. Put them in the freezer and freeze until hard. If using frozen strawberries, proceed from this point.

2 Just before serving, put the frozen strawberries in a large food processor with the sugar, vanilla extract and buttermilk. Blitz until smooth and serve immediately.

This has got to be one of the quickest desserts in the book. You can do it with frozen bananas, too: just have them ready-frozen, and this ice cream can be made and ready to eat in minutes. It contains hardly any fat and has such a fresh flavour. Buttermilk is the best liquid to use, but you can also use yoghurt, as it won't split while blending.

INSTANT STRAWBERRY ICE CREAM

Serves 4
100g oatmeal
300ml double cream
50ml whisky
400g raspberries
50g caster sugar
40ml crème de cassis

1 Toast the oatmeal in a dry frying pan over a medium heat for 1–2 minutes, until golden and nutty, then turn out and leave to cool.

2 Whip the cream to soft peaks with the whisky. Lightly crush half the raspberries with the sugar and swirl them through the cream, along with the oatmeal, to create a marbled effect.

3 Spoon the raspberry cream into a large glass bowl and top with the remaining raspberries. Spoon over the crème de cassis and serve.

Toasting the oatmeal is a must here, as is using good Scottish raspberries when they're in season. Raspberries are one of Scotland's great ingredients, some of the best you'll ever taste. Next time you're up there, try to buy a raspberry plant. I bought one from a fruit farm on the west coast, so now I have a little bit of Scotland in the bottom of my garden.

CRANACHAN WITH RASPBERRIES & CRÈME DE CASSIS

1 Preheat the grill to its highest setting. Hull and quarter the strawberries.

2 Make the sabayon. Place the egg yolks, sugar and vodka in a heatproof bowl set over a pan of barely simmering water. Whisk vigorously and constantly until the mixture becomes thick and foamy, then remove from the heat.

3 Place the strawberries in a heatproof dish. Spoon the sabayon over them, place under the grill and cook for 3 minutes, until golden brown. Serve immediately.

Serves 2
200g strawberries
3 egg yolks
1 tbsp caster sugar
1 tbsp vodka

This is so simple and tasty. Adding vodka to the sabayon isn't too overpowering when it's made into a pudding like this. You could add fresh basil or even tarragon to make a change. One thing's for sure, make it with fresh British strawberries in season – only then will you understand just how good they are.

STRAWBERRIES WITH VODKA SABAYON

STRAWBERRIES, SHORTBREAD & CREAM

Who doesn't like this combination? I saw it being made for the cover of a food magazine in the US. 'It's kind of like a scone,' I said to the woman preparing it for the shoot. 'No way!' she said. 'It's a shortbread!' As I was running late for my plane, I decided not to argue. But either way, it tastes good, and it's quick and easy.

Serves 8

250g cold butter, plus extra for greasing

250g caster sugar

150g cornflour

300g plain flour, plus extra for dusting

600g strawberries

1 vanilla pod

600ml double cream

1 Preheat the oven to 170°C/325°F/Gas mark 3. Cut the butter into cubes and lightly grease a baking tray.

2 In a large food processor, blitz the butter, 150g sugar, the cornflour and flour for 1–2 minutes, until well combined.

3 Turn out onto a lightly floured work surface and roll into a large sausage shape. Slice the sausage into 5mm thick discs. Place on the prepared tray and bake for 8–10 minutes. Remove and transfer to a wire rack to cool.

4 While the shortbreads are cooking, hull the strawberries and cut them in half. Split the vanilla pod in half lengthways and scrape out the seeds.

5 Whip the cream to soft peaks with the remaining sugar and the vanilla seeds.

6 To serve, divide the strawberries among 8 small bowls, top with the whipped cream and serve 2 biscuits alongside.

Makes 12
200g soft butter
200g caster sugar
4 eggs
200g self-raising flour, sifted

For the icing
200g soft butter
300g icing sugar, sifted
100g strawberry purée
sprinkles, to decorate

1 Preheat the oven to 180°C/350°F/Gas mark 4. Place 12 paper cases in a muffin tin.

2 Beat the butter and sugar until white and fluffy, then beat in the eggs one at a time. Fold in the flour, then divide the mixture between the paper cases.

3 Bake the cupcakes for 10–12 minutes, then leave to cool on a wire rack.

4 Meanwhile, to make the icing, whisk together the butter, icing sugar and strawberry purée.

5 Once cooled slightly, spread the cupcakes with the strawberry icing and decorate with the sprinkles.

Cupcakes are absolutely everywhere in America, and have become pretty common elsewhere too, especially with young people. It's always a popular dessert for anyone with a sweet tooth. This is the British way of making them, which I prefer to the American method of using corn oil and corn syrup. Butter tastes much better.

STRAWBERRY CUPCAKES

1 Preheat the oven to 200°C/400°F/Gas mark 6. Grease 4 ovenproof ramekins generously with butter, then coat the insides with some of the caster sugar, tapping out the excess.

2 Cut the passion fruits in half and scoop out the seeds. Whisk the seeds and juice into the custard.

3 Whisk the egg whites to stiff peaks with the remaining sugar. Fold them into the passion fruit-custard mixture.

4 Divide the mixture among the prepared ramekins and bake for 8–10 minutes, until risen and golden. Dust with icing sugar and serve immediately.

Serves 4
soft butter, for greasing
4 tbsp caster sugar
4 passion fruits
150ml fresh ready-made custard
4 egg whites
1 tsp icing sugar

This has got to be one of the best shortcuts in the book: just shop-bought custard with a few egg whites and some passion fruits, and it works every time, I promise. You won't be worrying about cooking soufflés any more when you see how easy this really is.

INSTANT PASSION FRUIT SOUFFLÉ

Serves 4
200ml double cream
25ml milk
30g icing sugar
juice of 1 lemon, strained
100ml limoncello, very cold

1 Whisk all the ingredients together in a bowl until smooth. Divide among 4 small serving glasses and place in the fridge to chill.

2 Serve with a glass of limoncello on the side.

Posset has to be one of the easiest desserts to make. The idea is that the lemon juice sets the cream, and whisking it a little will speed up the process. Limoncello is a great liqueur from the west coast of Italy, mainly Amalfi, which is one of the most beautiful parts of the world. As well being famous for its coastline, it's known for the lemons that grow on the hills. Limoncello is traditionally made with lemon zest that's steeped in grain alcohol until the oils are released, then combined with a simple sugar syrup. It's always best served very cold.

LEMON POSSET WITH LIMONCELLO

SPICED CHARRED PINEAPPLE WITH ICE CREAM

This idea came from when we were just messing around in the kitchen one night, looking for a garnish to go with something. It worked so well that I had to include it here, and thanks to my chef Chris for this one. I stopped him when he started chopping chillies to go on top of it, though!

Serves 4
1 pineapple
100g caster sugar
2 tsp ground mixed spice
2 limes
*4 scoops vanilla ice cream,
to serve*

1 Peel and core the pineapple, and cut it into 12 long wedges. Remove the inner core if it's tough. Mix together the sugar and mixed spice.

2 Heat a ridged griddle pan until hot. Sprinkle the spice and sugar mixture over the pineapple pieces, place them on the griddle pan and cook for 2–3 minutes on each side, until charred. Turn them with tongs.

3 Halve the limes and add them, cut-side down, for the last minute of cooking time.

4 Serve 3 slices of pineapple and a scoop of ice cream per person, with half a charred lime to squeeze over.

WARM CHOCOLATE & MARSHMALLOW COOKIES

I've brought so many great recipes from the US, and this is one of them. I've changed it a bit though, as American recipes often don't work over here, because the flour is different and they use a lot of corn oil and corn syrup there. So, this is the Anglicized version of Miss Simpson's cookies from Connecticut.

Makes 12

225g soft butter,
plus extra for greasing

350g plain flour, plus extra
for dusting

1 tsp bicarbonate of soda

1 tsp salt

175g caster sugar

175g soft brown sugar

1 tsp vanilla extract

2 eggs, beaten

350g chocolate chips or
chopped nuts

100g small marshmallows

1 Preheat the oven to 180°C/350°F/Gas mark 4 and grease 2 baking trays.

2 In a large stand mixer, mix the flour, bicarbonate of soda, salt, butter, sugars, vanilla and eggs, and blitz until well mixed. Add the chocolate chips or nuts and mix again briefly.

3 Tip the mixture out onto a lightly floured work surface and divide into 12 evenly sized balls. Place on the baking trays, well spaced out, flatten down slightly and bake for 9–11 minutes, until golden and just set.

4 After 6 minutes of cooking time, remove from the oven and top with the marshmallow pieces, then return to the oven.

5 Allow to cool slightly on the trays, then serve warm.

1 Preheat the oven to 180°C/350°F/Gas mark 4. Place 12 paper cases in a muffin tin.

2 Using a stand mixer, beat the butter and sugar until white and fluffy, then beat in the eggs one at a time. Fold in the flour, then divide among the paper cases. Bake in the oven for 10–12 minutes, then set aside to cool a little.

3 Meanwhile, make the icing. Mix together the sugar and a little cold water in a pan to make a paste. Place the pan on the hob and bring to the boil, then simmer until it reaches 121°C/250°F on a sugar thermometer. This is soft ball stage; if you don't have a thermometer you can drop a little syrup into a glass of cold water, and it should form a soft ball.

Makes 12
200g soft butter
200g caster sugar
4 eggs
200g self-raising flour

For the icing
150g caster sugar
3 egg whites
150g very soft butter
icing sugar, for dusting

4 While the sugar is simmering, whisk the egg whites to stiff peaks in the mixer. When the sugar is ready, carefully pour the sugar onto the whites while continuing to whisk. Once all the sugar is mixed in, keep whisking until the meringue is cold.

5 Dice the soft butter into cubes and beat it into the icing until smooth. Transfer it to a piping bag.

6 Cut a small circle out of the top of the cooled cakes and cut the circle in half to make the wings. Pipe a swirl of icing into each cake and top with the 2 halves of cake pointing upwards. Dust with icing sugar to serve.

Here's one the Yanks can't call their own. The idea comes from an amazing bakery whose owners have been there for four generations. The old boy who bakes every day is 80, his commis chef is 76, and the shop has remained unchanged since it opened. These butterfly cakes reminded me of the ones my gran used to bake for me. They were so good I put them straight on my afternoon tea menu.

BUTTERFLY CAKES

WAFFLES WITH BACON & MAPLE SYRUP

Thomas Keller, one of the world's best chefs, came on my show a while ago and cooked waffles with chicken. I hadn't realized how easy they were to make before then, and I've been cooking them ever since. It's best to use American streaky bacon and good-quality maple syrup, which is graded like fine wine: the better the grade, the better the flavour. They can easily be cooked in ten minutes in a waffle maker, and the same batter can be used for both sweet and savoury waffles if you want to serve fruit, chocolate sauce or ice cream with them.

Serves 4
250g plain flour
1 tbsp baking powder
1 tsp salt
1 tbsp caster sugar
3 eggs
425ml milk
100g butter, melted
vegetable oil, for greasing
streaky bacon rashers, to serve
maple syrup, to serve

1 Whisk the flour, baking powder, salt, sugar, eggs, milk and butter together in a bowl to make a smooth batter with no lumps.

2 Oil a waffle maker, pour in the batter and cook for 3–4 minutes. Remove and keep warm. Repeat to make more waffles.

3 Meanwhile, heat a frying pan over a medium-high heat, add the bacon and cook until crispy. Remove and keep warm.

4 Serve the waffles hot with the bacon and maple syrup.

BLACKBERRY & MAPLE SYRUP PANCAKES

O'Rourkes diner in Middletown, Connecticut, is famous for being one of the first diners in the US that's still going. The menu is massive, as are the portions, but neither are as massive as the guy who runs it. Brian is the true star of the show. They serve 40-odd types of egg dishes listed on a seven-page menu. But best of all are the pancakes with fruit and maple syrup.

Serves 4

200g plain flour
10g baking powder
2 eggs
200ml milk
vegetable oil, for frying
100ml maple syrup
400g blackberries

1 Whisk together the flour, baking powder, eggs and milk in a bowl to make a smooth batter.

2 To make the pancakes, heat a little oil in a non-stick frying pan. Spoon the mixture into the pan using a dessertspoon. Cook in batches for 1–2 minutes, or until the edges of the pancakes are slightly brown. Flip them over and cook on the other side. Remove and keep warm.

3 Meanwhile, gently warm through the maple syrup and blackberries in a saucepan for 1–2 minutes.

4 Serve the pancakes warm with several spoonfuls of the blackberries and syrup.

Makes 10

80g butter, melted, plus extra for greasing
275g self-raising flour
1 tsp bicarbonate of soda
½ tsp salt
150ml buttermilk
150ml milk
150g granulated sugar
2 eggs
250ml double cream
3 passion fruits
icing sugar, for dusting

1 Preheat the oven 180°C/350°F/Gas mark 4. Lightly grease a whoopie-cake tin or shallow bun tin.

2 In a bowl, whisk together the flour, bicarbonate of soda, salt, buttermilk, milk, butter, sugar and eggs to make a smooth batter. Divide among the tins and bake for 10 minutes, or until risen and golden. Remove from the oven and leave to cool on a wire rack.

3 Meanwhile, whip the cream to soft peaks. Cut the passion fruits in half, scoop out the seeds and fold them in.

4 Sandwich 2 whoopie cake halves together with the passion fruit cream, then repeat with the rest of the cakes. Dust with icing sugar and serve.

If I told you the story of how I learned to make these, you wouldn't believe me. It involved a neighbourhood called Dumbo and a flat right under Manhattan Bridge in Brooklyn, New York City, followed by a whoopie party. There were lots of other things too, but these were ace, and far better than cupcakes. You can buy special whoopie tins online, or shallow Yorkshire pudding or bun tins work well. You can also bake them on a normal baking tray using an ice-cream scoop to shape the mixture, as the cakes keep their shape well.

PASSION FRUIT WHOOPIE CAKES

INDEX

Acknowledgements

Firstly, I'd like to thank the entire team at Quadrille for doing an amazing job on this new book, and for working tirelessly to get it all into shape. Thanks to Laura and Jane for making it happen, and to Gabriella for making it all look like it's happened! Cheers to Tara and Sue for working at my place for three weeks, and for dog-sitting in between taking the fantastic pictures for the book.

Thanks to my team – Chris, Sam and Louise – for going above and beyond in order to get the book done, and for all the washing up. Oh, and to Fudge and Ralph, my boys – thank you for eating all the leftover bits that dropped on the floor.

Thank you to everyone for watching the shows I continue to make. I'll always try my best, each and every day, to make a difference. Thank you, and I hope you enjoy the new book.